Bento Love

By Kentaro Kobayashi

Photography by Hideo Sawai

VERTICAL.

Contents

Numbers in parentheses indicate recipe page

Introduction

This book is written with the person on the receiving end of the bento box in mind. It's chock full of recipes that growing boys and girls (or the young at heart) actually want to eat. So you won't find any cutesy, time-consuming and elaborate recipes and designs that characterize the typical Japanese lunch box. No little decorative picks or meaningless frills that get in the way when you try to put the lid on. This book is realistic, and above all prioritizes the cravings of the hungry student or worker bee over the artistic urges of the bento maker. Of course, I also included plenty of helpful hints for creating bento as well.

There are certainly many things about bento that I only noticed once I entered the kitchen and started making my own bento lunches. My mother put all kinds of creative and considerate touches into the bento she made for me, which I never noticed when I was just a kid.

Nonetheless, I chose to write this book from the less enlightened perspective of the lunch box eater. After all, I can't help being particularly fond of the bento tradition. Until just recently, these delicious and nutritious portable Japanese meals were the sunshine that brightened my day.

Looking back, I now recognize that my mother Katsuyo made elegantly simple bento with healthy servings of vegetables, filled with the wisdom and love of a parent who was also a true master chef. But truthfully, when I was a meat-addicted young man, I secretly longed for less vegetables and more proteins. I still clearly remember those secret cravings. So when it comes to bento, even though I'm now a professional chef, my preferences are still childlike. So here I present big and meaty bento that keep in touch with the hungry kid at heart. You won't find bento that are mostly vegetable-rich side dishes. Here you'll find hearty, heaping servings of meat. They're sure to encourage hungry kids to gobble all that rice right down. That's the kind of bento you'll find in this book.

A bento is a lunch in a box. As the cook stands in the kitchen making a portable meal for her child or spouse, he or she usually considers nutritional balance, personal preferences and other factors. Certainly, lunch, in a box or otherwise, constitutes one of the three major meals of the day. But that doesn't mean it has to be a perfectly balanced serving of vitamins, minerals, protein and carbohydrates. It doesn't have to be a colorful and ingeniously creative expression of one's love. My approach to bento is somewhere in between the instant Western lunch and the love-filled but labor-intensive Japanese bento.

After all, the love is always there but sometimes the time or energy isn't. Countless Japanese mothers are often forced to rely on frozen foods or just hand over lunch money. And that's no big deal. You can always heap on the vegetables at dinner to make up for any afternoon nutritional loss. Or, whip up a quick vegetable stir-fry to go with eggs at breakfast. Or pass the veggie juice.

Daily nutritional balance is important, but bento is just one meal in the day, and in my opinion, it doesn't have to be too special. I definitely recommend trying the heart-filled and healthy bento habit, but feel free to think of it as a lunch like any other. It can be as simple or as fancy as you like, just so long as the overall nutritional intake for the day balances out.

In fact, my bento style presents a good opportunity to subtly encourage meat-craving youngsters to eat their veggies, too. Teens may want a purely protein afternoon meal, but give them what they want, and they will surely discover after some meat and rice, a little vegetable on the side is pretty tasty after all. Just say, "Isn't this broccoli delicious? I simply boiled it. It's all in the seasoning!" So forget the pressure. There's no need to show off. Don't worry about putting in extra time. But do make these bento with a big heart. Emphasis on *big*.

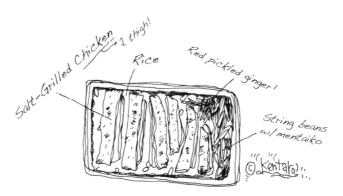

Salt-Grilled Chicken —1 thigh!
Rice
Red pickled ginger!
String beans w/ mentaiko
©Kentaro

I always dreamed of having steak for lunch.

For me, the moment right before I opened the bento box lid was the most exciting. Just thinking, what if a steak is waiting in there...
If my experience is any example, I think that young growing teens with a hankering for meat have dreams of juicy steak for lunch.
I wrote this chapter with the intention of making those dreams come true. Here I introduce four dreamy steak lunches.
All of them are impressively heavy on the meat.

Dreamy Steak Bento

Deluxe Steak Bento
Cook it, slice it, top it — *Ta-da!*

Steak for bento should always be well-done. Coat with soy sauce while sizzling hot and quickly slide onto the rice.

Steak for lunch is truly a dream come true. Don't forget, though, that bento are eaten a couple of hours after they're made, so it is essential to cook meat well. So "cover and cook" is the key! Coat a well-heated pan with oil. Add meat, sprinkle with a dash of salt and soy sauce and fire away over high heat until browned. Flip meat over and cover. Heat's on high the whole time, by the way. Steak is done when no juice comes out when a skewer is inserted. Once cooked, cut into strips and dunk each sizzling strip one by one into soy sauce. Slide the steak strips onto freshly steamed rice. Having rice ready and waiting is rule number one in bento box preparation. Combine with sautéed watercress and sweet simmered shiitake mushrooms. Add oil to a well-heated pan, and quickly sauté halved watercress. Season with salt, soy sauce and pepper. Add extra oil and stir-fry two halved fresh shiitake mushrooms. Once cooked, add 1/2 tsp each soy sauce and mirin, simmer, and stir to coat. Make the side dishes before cooking steak and you can prepare the whole bento with just one pan.

**Beef Steak
+
Simmered Shiitake Mushrooms
+
Sautéed Watercress**

Layered Steak
+
Sautéed Corn
+
Boiled Okra
+
Seasoned Wakame Seaweed
+
Pickled Plum

Layered Steak Bento

**Layer thinly sliced beef, grill it, and *voilà*!
A lovely steak lunch.**

**Finish with a sprinkle of soy sauce.
Corn fried in the steak juices is also delicious!**

Let me introduce to you my secret technique for enjoying the sensation of steak using thinly sliced beef. Use 6 slices (3 1/2 oz (100 g) total) thinly sliced lean beef. Stack three slices together and fry. This gives you a crispy on the outside, juicy on the inside, delicious layered steak. Be sure to press the beef slices down well so they don't break up while frying.

To Cook: Coat a well-heated pan with oil. Add two layered steaks. Sprinkle with a dash of salt and pepper and fry both sides over high heat until well browned and deliciously crispy. Pour in 1 Tbsp soy sauce, stir to coat, and it's finished. Remove meat and sauté corn in the same pan. Use 3 Tbsp whole corn kernels. Stir-fry over medium high heat. Corn sautéed in savory steak juices is a tasty treat that will truly get your tummy rumbling. Slice layered steak into bite-size pieces. Fill the lunch box with steak, corn, and 5 okra boiled in salted water. You can serve the steak on top of rice, too, if you like.

Pork Steak Bento
Sesame oil and ginger make this steak great!

Soak in sauce after frying.
The sesame oil sauce is guaranteed
to get your mouth watering.

Pork can hold its own in the world of steaks.
However, clumps of fat appear when chilled if
too greasy, so pick a lean cut. I use a single slab
(3 1/2 oz (100 g) total) of pork shoulder meat.
The key is immediately dipping the sizzling steak
in the sesame sauce (1 Tbsp soy sauce, 1/3 tsp
sesame oil, grated ginger to taste). The effect of
this sauce is just amazing. It truly takes the flavor
to a whole new level.

To prepare: Coat a well-heated pan with oil, add
pork, sprinkle with salt and soy sauce, and sauté
until lightly browned. Turn meat over, cover, and
reduce heat. Cook slowly until no juices come out
when poked with a skewer. Soak pork in sauce
for at least 5 minutes. Slice and add to lunch
box.

Packing Tips: Serve with sautéed snap peas and
shimeji (clamshell) mushrooms. Coat a heated
pan with oil, add as many snap peas as you like
and sauté over medium heat. Season with salt
and pepper. Next, add 1/2 pack *shimeji* mushrooms, shredding by hand. Stir-fry over medium
heat. Season with soy sauce and Japanese
sansho pepper. Ordinary black pepper may be
substituted.

Pork Steak
+
Sautéed Snap Peas and
Shimeji Mushrooms
+
Shiba-style Pickles
(pickled eggplant)

Salt-Grilled Chicken
+
String Beans
with *Mentaiko*
+
Toasted Seaweed
+
Red Pickled Ginger

Salt-Grilled Chicken Steak Bento

Extra salty flavor goes great with cold rice

Keep in mind, chicken cooks slowly.
So don't forget to cover and let it cook through.

Enjoy the flavor of yakitori-style chicken for lunch! But don't forget, chicken must be cooked really, really well. Take a single chicken thigh (8 3/4 oz (250 g)) and poke about a dozen holes through the skin with a knife for even cooking and to prevent skin from shriveling up. Remove fat with cooking scissors and slice the surface of the meat repeatedly to break up tendons. Rub a very generous amount of salt (about 1 Tbsp) into both sides and sprinkle with pepper. Now you're ready to cook.

Add oil to a well-heated pan and place chicken in skin-side down. Fry over high heat until skin is crispy and charred. Flip, reduce heat to medium, cover and cook slowly until no juices (or only clear liquid) comes out when poked with a skewer. Turn heat to high and cook both sides for a crisped finish. Slice and serve on top of rice covered with toasted seaweed. Finish with seven-spice or cayenne powder, if desired. Serve with red pickled ginger and string beans with *mentaiko* (recipe on page 87).

A Little Note about Useful Cooking Supplies, Bento Boxes, and Various Other Things

Spices and Seasonings

The items listed here come in handy when making any-thing, not just bento. So be sure to keep your kitchen well-stocked.

First recommendation: *Sesame Oil*

I am so hopelessly in love with the smooth and rich flavor of sesame oil that I am helpless without it. It goes great with just about every vegetable or meat. And it's a perfect match for rice, too. It goes without saying that it's indispensable in stir-fried dishes, but it's just as tasty simply sprinkled on boiled veggies. A little sesame oil can draw out depths of flavor even the ingredients themselves didn't know they had. Plain vegetable oil just can't compare. In any case, sesame oil is a definite must-have.

Next on the list: *Cracked Sesame Seeds and Roasted Sesame Seeds*

These two members of the sesame family are also good friends of mine. I love their heart-warming fragrance, and they make whatever they are sprinkled on look good, too. Just add sesame, and even plain rice becomes a stylish and satisfying treat. And as if that weren't enough, sesame is good for your health, too. I am forever indebted to both black and white sesame seeds.

Another useful item: *Curry Powder*

Dress boiled veggies in curry powder and rice vinegar, add a pinch of salt and pepper, and *voilà*, you have yourself an instant curry marinade. Add a little of this luscious spice to a stir-fry, and the same old dish becomes an exciting new entrée. Curry powder goes great with soy sauce, too, and makes rice all the more tempting.

Yet another useful item: *Chili Powder*

Chili powder is a mixed spice consisting of powdered chili peppers, oregano, dill, and other spices. Seven-spice powder is a similar mix that's more common in Asia. Often used in Mexican cuisine, chili powder goes great with meat dishes. And with mayonnaise, too. Chili powder mayonnaise is fabulous. Be careful not to confuse this spice with chili pepper.

Not to be neglected: *Other Herbs and Spices*

For starters, at least keep basil and oregano on hand. Dried versions are fine. They don't have to be fresh, but they do have to be there when you need them. Add them to stir-fries, salads, marinades, anything. You don't have to get particularly picky about how and when to use them, just trust your instincts. It's said that herbs also help prevent food from going bad, but I recommend them mostly for flavor. When using herbs, use olive oil. Its strong yet subtle flavor suits these Mediterranean spices.

Preserves and Other Food Products

Japanese pickles, dried foods, tsukudani, etc.

Red pickled ginger. Pickled plums, certainly. *Shiba*-style pickled cucumbers and eggplants, *takuan* pickled daikon, the list goes on. All of them are quick and excellent additions to bento. Japanese pickles are something you'll definitely want to keep around, and are generally available in Asian markets. Dried and preserved foods such as dried young sardines (*shirasu*) and sweet soy sauce-simmered ingredients (*tsukudani*) like kelp or baby fish also keep well and are good instant sides. Try to keep a variety of these preserved foods on hand. They make white rice a tasty treat without any trouble. Do take the time, though, to wipe excess moisture from pickles with a paper towel before adding them to the bento box.

Cheese, another versatile lunch box addition

Potatoes sprinkled with Parmesan, sandwiches made with sliced cheese. Cheese makes a nice and easy addition to any lunch box. Little servings of individually wrapped cheeses are welcome treats, too. Avoid creamy cheeses that melt easily. For bento, processed cheese works well.

About Bento Boxes and Accessories

When picking a bento box, you'll want to find one with a tight fitting lid that doesn't let liquids leak. As for the little foil trays and plastic picks often used to separate and serve sides, you need quite a few to get through the week, so I'd rather avoid them altogether. All the garbage is a pain, and bad for the environment, too. Just focus on the food itself. If you have some sides that might clash flavor-wise, try separating them with a serving of simple boiled veggies. If you cook your dishes properly so they don't get all drippy or mushy, then you don't have to worry too much about keeping them to themselves. Pick a cute bento box, use good quality spices, keep your pantry stocked with preserved foods, and in no time you will become a bento master.

Shiba-style Pickle

Bento Loves Fried Meat Dishes

In this chapter, I will introduce to you a parade of meat-filled recipes that work well in everyday bento. All of them are prepared in the same way—stir-fried. Fast, easy and delicious, there's no better way to whip up a delicious dish.

When making stir-fry for bento you want to be careful to cook meat thoroughly, whether it's pork, beef, or poultry. And choose lean meat, since unattractive clumps form in fatty meat when cooled.

As for vegetables, use high heat and stir-fry quickly so the dish doesn't get soggy later.

If the dish gets watery when cooking, though, don't fret. Just drain off the water, add more oil, and give it another pass over high heat.

By the way, many of these recipes use the phrase "well-heated pan," but that's in the case of a cast-iron pan. If you are using a Teflon pan, you don't need to get it too hot.

Pork and Cabbage Stir-fry Bento

The sauce is delicious even when chilled

Recipe on page 18

This dish contains the basic ingredients used in yaki-soba, but with rice instead of noodles. Be careful not to overcook the cabbage—keep it crispy. Simply slice up the *kabocha* and sauté it. That's all. Serve stir-fry and *kabocha* right next to the rice, and don't worry if the sauces blend together. It's tasty that way.

Pork and Cabbage Stir-fry
+
Sautéed *Kabocha*
+
Red Pickled Ginger

17

Pork and Cabbage Stir-fry Bento

Don't overcook cabbage and keep the sauce under control

Photo on page 17

Pork and Cabbage Stir-fry

Ingredients
3 1/2 oz (100 g) thinly sliced lean pork
2 cabbage leaves
Dash each salt and pepper
1 Tbsp Worcestershire sauce
2 tsp vegetable oil

Instructions
1. Cut pork and cabbage into bite-size pieces.
2. Add oil to a heated pan and stir-fry pork over medium heat.
3. When pork turns brown, add cabbage and stir-fry briefly. Sprinkle with salt and pepper. When cabbage is cooked season with Worcestershire sauce.

Packing Tips: Serve with Sautéed *Kabocha*. The buttery flavor goes great with sauce-coated meat. Garnish rice with red pickled ginger.

Side Dish: Sautéed *Kabocha*

Cut as much *kabocha* (Japanese pumpkin) as you like into 1/5" (5 mm) thick slices. In a pan, heat a small amount of butter over low heat just until melted. Place pumpkin in pan and cook both sides on medium low heat until lightly browned. *Kabocha* is done when a skewer can be easily inserted. Sprinkle with salt, pepper, and if desired, cinnamon. Slicing *kabocha* thinly is key. Also, watch the heat. If you use too much heat it'll burn.

Spicy Miso Pork Stir-fry Bento

First meat, then veggies, and finish with miso sauce

Photo on page 20

Spicy Miso Pork Stir-fry

Ingredients
3 1/2 oz (100 g) thinly sliced pork thigh
1 green bell pepper
1/2 small carrot
Miso sauce:
   1/2 Tbsp each miso, mirin (sweet cooking wine), sake
   1/2 tsp Doubanjiang (Chinese chili paste)
Pepper, to taste
2 tsp sesame oil

Instructions
1. Cut pork into bite-size pieces. Deseed green pepper and cut lengthwise into thin strips. Peel carrot and slice into 1/5" (5 mm) half-moon slices. Combine miso sauce ingredients.
2. Add sesame oil to a well-heated pan and stir-fry pork over medium heat.
3. When pork is lightly browned, add carrot, stir-fry, then add green pepper. Stir-fry again.
4. When everything is cooked, pour miso sauce into pan and stir over high heat. Finish with freshly ground pepper. If you don't have a pepper grinder, you can use powdered pepper, but fresh-ground is best.

Packing Tips: Serve with Rolled Omelet. It has a nice hint of soy sauce. Top rice with a refreshing pickled plum.

Note: Combine miso sauce ingredients ahead of time. Add extra Doubanjiang if you like, but be careful—it gets spicy!

Side Dish: Rolled Omelet

Stir 1 egg just enough to blend white and yolk, add 1/2 to 1 tsp sugar and a dash of soy sauce. Mix well. Spread oil thinly over a heated pan and add 1/3 egg mixture. Spread egg evenly over pan surface. Once the egg is cooked through, roll up omelet from one edge until it's resting on the opposite side of the pan. Pour 1/2 of remaining egg onto open pan surface. Cook until half-done and roll, wrapping first omelet inside. Repeat last step with remaining egg mixture.

**Spicy Miso
Pork Stir-fry
+
Rolled Omelet
+
Pickled Plum**

Spicy Miso Pork Stir-fry Bento

Simple yet sublime, and a mouth-watering match for rice

Recipe on page 19

Sometimes it's nice to spice things up a bit. Mix miso and Doubanjiang for a tasty tongue-tingling sensation. When stir-frying vegetables, wait a bit between carrots and green peppers. The time lapse ensures that everything gets cooked just right. This kind of minor detail makes a big difference. Also, for the rolled omelet, don't worry about using a special omelet skillet. An ordinary frying pan works just fine.

Zha Cai and Pork Stir-fry Bento

Great with turnip greens!

Recipe on page 22

Using pickles like Sichuan vegetable, or *zha cai*, in stir-fry works really well for bento. However, Sichuan vegetable has a very strong aroma so be sure to rinse it thoroughly. Don't worry about losing flavor, those crunchy little guys are plenty tasty even after rinsing. As for the meat, slice thinly along the grain, along the tendons. This keeps meat from falling apart when stir-fried. Top rice with salted turnip greens. Turnip greens on rice is a delicious dish in and of itself. Yum.

**_Zha Cai_ and
Pork Stir-fry
+
Fish Cake
+
Salted Turnip
Greens**

Zha Cai and Pork Stir-fry Bento

Rinse Sichuan vegetable well before adding to the stir-fry!

Photo on page 21

Zha Cai and Pork Stir-fry

Ingredients

3 1/2 oz (100 g) thinly sliced pork thigh
1 oz (30 g) *zha cai* (Sichuan vegetable)
Dash each salt and pepper
White sesame seeds, to taste
1 tsp soy sauce
2 tsp sesame oil

Instructions

1. Slice pork thinly along the grain, about 1/5"
   (5 mm) thick. Cut *zha cai* into thin strips and
   rinse thoroughly. Squeeze dry.
2. Add sesame oil to a well-heated pan. Add pork
   and season with salt and pepper. Sauté over
   medium high. When pork turns brown, add
   zha cai. Stir-fry vigorously. Season with soy
   sauce and sprinkle with sesame seeds.

Packing Tips: Serve with Salted Turnip Greens.
Turnip greens on rice goes great with the main
dish, and with fish cakes, too. Cut about 5
slices of fish cake and pack directly into lunch
box. The mild flavor provides a refreshing treat
between tasty mouthfuls of strongly flavored pork
stir-fry. Give it a try.

Side Dish: Salted Turnip Greens

Rinse 1 bunch turnip greens and spread in
a colander. Douse with boiling hot water and
squeeze to drain. Chop finely and sprinkle
1/2 tsp salt. Rub in salt until greens "sweat."
Thoroughly squeeze out excess moisture. Add
another 1/2 tsp salt and mix in, allowing flavor
to be absorbed. Any leftover salted turnip
greens can be used as a side dish for the
evening meal.

Kentaro's *Once Upon a Bento* Story

The bento my mother made were simple and delicious.

Bento filled with a variety of colorful side dishes jostling for attention, bento with beautiful edible works of art resting on top of rice, bento filled with sausages cut into cute little shapes—these kinds of bento lunch boxes were not to be found in the Kobayashi household. My mother Katsuyo made lunches that were meant to be a feast for the stomach, not for the eyes.

A carefully cooked main dish accompanied by a healthy serving of seasonal vegetables. That's the kind of bento my mother made. My sister, father and I all ate the same Katsuyo Kobayashi-style lunch. There was no distinction between boy and girl or kid and adult. In the evenings we would wash our own bento box. That was the daily routine.

But it was a different story on field trip days and special school events. The usual simple, healthy menu was transformed into a deluxe lunch that occupied my mind all day. I should make it clear, though, that when I say "deluxe" I am using a very personal standard of evaluation. The contents of the Katsuyo Kobayashi deluxe bento were as follows: rice balls, fried chicken, a rolled omelet, a serving of some simmered dish, and a seasonal green vegetable. Calling this deluxe might give the impression that my family was conservative or very stingy. But you have to understand that both rice balls and fried chicken were special favorites for us kids. For kids (of all ages) nothing is more luxurious than your favorite food. It's not a matter of expense, although chicken wasn't cheap. It was a rare occasion when we had fried chicken at our house. And rice balls never showed up in the usual daily bento menu.

That's where my mother was clever. She didn't easily give in to our cravings. But when it came time for a special event, she went all out and gave us our favorites. Thanks to my mother's strategy of saving special dishes for special events, even now that I am grown and can make for myself whatever I want whenever I want to, I still have special respect for fried chicken. Ah, but it truly brings back memories. How I looked forward to those deluxe bento!

Beef and Green Pepper Stir-fry Bento

A Chinese favorite, packed with fresh green peppers

Recipe on page 26

This dish is standard fare for growing kids, and is especially popular with boys. I had a friend who used to bring it for lunch every day. The trick is to stir-fry quickly and energetically. If you take your time it will turn to mush. And don't forget the oyster sauce. Oyster sauce is great stuff. Versatile, goes well with beef, and lets you add a hint of authentic Chinese flavor. Garlic is optional, so if you are worried about odor, feel free to leave it out.

**Beef and Green Pepper
Stir-fry
+
Boiled Bean Sprouts
+
Pickled Plum**

**Spicy Sweet Beef
and Shiitake Stir-fry
+
Parboiled Rapini
+
Shiba-style Pickles**

Spicy Sweet Beef and Shiitake Stir-fry Bento

**Sweet, salty, and a must
on the list of lunch box
regulars—be generous
with the shiitake**

Recipe on page 27

Richly flavorful sweet and savory
sauce is perfect for bento boxes.
This dish is easy to make, but it can
be easily influenced by your mood.
It can easily get too salty or too
sweet. If you get caught up adding a
little more of this and that, you may
find yourself in a hot spot, literally.
So when you add seasonings, turn
off the heat first and take your time.

Beef and Green Pepper Stir-fry Bento
Use medium high heat from start to finish
Photo on page 24

Beef and Green Pepper Stir-fry

Ingredients

3 1/2 oz (100 g) thinly sliced lean beef
1 large green pepper
1/2 clove garlic
1/2 nub ginger
Salt and pepper, to taste
1 tsp oyster sauce
1 tsp soy sauce
2 tsp sesame oil

Instructions

1. Cut beef into bite-size pieces. Deseed green pepper and cut lengthwise into thin strips. Mince garlic and ginger.
2. Add sesame oil to a well-heated pan and sauté garlic and ginger until fragrant. Add beef and sauté over medium high heat.
3. When meat is lightly browned, add green peppers. Lightly season with salt and pepper and stir-fry.
4. When green peppers are tender quickly pour in oyster sauce and soy sauce. Stir and coat.

Packing Tips: Serve with Bean Sprouts with Fish Flakes, a great match for the strong flavor of oyster sauce. Top rice with a large pickled plum.

Side Dish: Bean Sprouts with Fish Flakes

Blanch a handful of bean sprouts and drain. Add a dash of soy sauce and bonito flakes and mix well. Drain thoroughly before adding to bento box.

Spicy Sweet Beef and Shiitake Stir-fry Bento

Stir-fry quickly after adding seasonings

Photo on page 25

Spicy Sweet Beef and Shiitake Stir-fry

Ingredients

3 1/2 oz (100 g) thinly sliced lean beef
2 shiitake mushrooms (fresh)
1/2 nub ginger
1 tsp each sugar, mirin (sweet cooking wine)
2 light tsp soy sauce
Japanese (*sansho*) pepper (or black pepper)
2 tsp sesame oil

Instructions

1. Cut beef into bite-size pieces. Remove stalks of shiitake and slice in half. Mince peeled ginger.
2. Add sesame oil to a well-heated pan and sauté beef over medium high heat.
3. When meat is lightly browned add shiitake and stir-fry. Add ginger, sugar, soy sauce, and mirin. Mix quickly.
4. Simmer on high heat and stir to coat. Finish with pepper.

Packing Tips: Serve with Blanched Rapini. The light refreshing flavor of fresh vegetables complements the thick, rich flavor of the main dish. It doesn't have to be rapini. Any seasonal green vegetable will do. Pack greens next to meat and top rice with *shiba*-style pickles.

Side Dish: Blanched Rapini

Blanch 2 to 3 stems of rapini in salted boiling water. Transfer to lukewarm water to remove bitterness, drain, and squeeze out excess water. Cut into bite-size pieces and lightly sprinkle with soy sauce.

Sesame Beef Bento

Whet your appetite with simple sesame flavor

Recipe on page 30

Stir-fried in sesame oil and sprinkled with sesame seeds, this dish is a richly flavored treat that's a snap to make. A heaping serving of this kind of beef is actually the very thing kids want to find in their lunch box. The fact that you can whip it up in no time is another plus.

And use lean meat. Fatty meat is great freshly cooked, but gets unattractive clumps when chilled.

**Sesame Beef
+
Komatsuna with
Young Sardines
+
Tsukudani Kelp**

Buttered Beef and Broccoli Bento

For butter sautéed beef the trick is to add a little oil

Recipe on page 31

Butter and soy sauce are a match made in heaven. However, when cooking with animal fat like butter, the dish clumps up when chilled. You can avoid this dilemma by adding a drop of vegetable oil. It's a great trick to remember. Broccoli added to stir-fry is tasty too.

Buttered Beef and Broccoli + Carrot Sticks

29

Sesame Beef Bento

Stir-fry in sesame oil, coat with sesame seeds and soy sauce—that's all it takes to make this dish delicious

Photo on page 28

Sesame Beef

Ingredients
3 1/2 oz (100 g) thinly sliced lean beef
Salt and pepper, to taste
White sesame seeds, to taste
1 light tsp soy sauce
2 tsp sesame oil

Instructions
1. Cut beef into bite-size pieces.
2. Add sesame oil to a well-heated pan and stir-fry beef over medium heat. Season with salt and pepper.
3. When meat is cooked, sprinkle with sesame seeds and soy sauce. Stir to coat.

Packing Tips: Serve with a refreshing green vegetable. Here, I use *komatsuna*, but seasonal greens like spinach or rapini work just as well. Add rice topped with *tsukudani* kelp (kelp stewed in soy sauce, mirin and sugar).

Side Dish: *Komatsuna* with Young Sardines

Boil 1/2 bundle of *komatsuna* (or spinach) in salted water, drain and soak in lukewarm water to remove bitterness. Squeeze out excess water. Cut to 1 1/2" (3 to 4 cm) lengths. Mix in 1 Tbsp dried young sardines (*shirasu*) and sprinkle with soy sauce.

Note: To make the most of the sesame flavor, use sesame oil, not vegetable oil, and be generous with the sesame seeds.

Buttered Beef and Broccoli Bento
Stir-fry beef in butter and oil, and add broccoli at the end
Photo on page 29

Beef and Broccoli Butter Sauté
Ingredients
3 1/2 oz (100 g) thinly sliced lean beef
1/2 bunch broccoli
Salt and pepper, to taste
1 tsp soy sauce
1/2 tsp vegetable oil
1/2 Tbsp butter

Instructions
1. Cut beef into bite-size pieces. Break broccoli up into small clusters and blanch in boiling water with salt added.
2. Add vegetable oil and butter to a heated pan and melt butter. Add beef, season with salt and pepper, and stir-fry over medium heat.
3. When meat turns brown, add boiled broccoli. Stir-fry quickly. When broccoli is coated with oil season with soy sauce.

Packing Tips: The main dish is packed full of beef and broccoli, so serve simple raw carrots on the side. Cut peeled carrots into 2 1/2" (6 to 7 cm) sticks and serve with mayonnaise for dipping. Sprinkle rice with black sesame seeds, if desired.

Note: Butter burns easily, so add meat when butter is partially melted and coat quickly.

Cashew Chicken Stir-fry Bento

A Chinese classic is great for lunch!

Recipe on page 34

It looks impressive, tastes delicious, and doesn't require any difficult techniques whatsoever. What more could you ask for? You might almost think it's a waste to serve this dish in a box for lunch, but don't worry about that. Anything that tastes good even cold is perfect for bento. Sure, this uses a lot of different ingredients, but don't let that keep you from giving it a try. If possible, use unsalted cashew nuts. But in a pinch, salted cashew nuts are okay too. Just reduce the amount of salt and soy sauce used when seasoning.

**Cashew Chicken
Stir-fry
+
Plum Dressed
Asparagus**

**Chicken and
Eggplant Stir-fry
+
Grilled Sweet
Peppers**

Chicken and Eggplant Stir-fry Bento

**Sprinkle with herbs,
season with soy sauce**

Recipe on page 35

It's said that herbs help prevent food from going bad. Plus, they go great with meat. So put them to use when making bento. Here, I use fragrant basil. Season with soy sauce for a salty flavor with an edge that still goes great with rice. Remove bitterness from eggplants by soaking in salted water. Cook chicken thoroughly by covering and steaming.

Cashew Chicken Stir-fry Bento

Cut chicken and veggies to match cashew nuts for a scrumptious-looking crunchy chunky dish

Photo on page 32

Cashew Chicken Stir-fry

Ingredients

3 1/2 oz (100 g) chicken
1/2 green bell pepper
1 3/4 oz (50 g) boiled bamboo shoot
1/2 clove garlic
1/2 nub ginger
1/2 C cashew nuts (plain)
1 tsp soy sauce
1 tsp oyster sauce
Salt and pepper, to taste
2 tsp sesame oil

Instructions

1. Dice chicken, deseeded green pepper and bamboo shoot into 2/5" (1 cm) cubes. Mince garlic and ginger.
2. Add sesame oil to a well-heated pan and sauté chicken, garlic and ginger over medium heat. Season with salt and pepper.
3. When chicken is cooked, add green pepper, bamboo shoot, and cashew nuts. Stir-fry.
4. Add soy sauce and oyster sauce and coat quickly.

Packing Tips: Pack a heaping portion of cashew chicken stir-fry in a compartment all by itself.
Serve Plum Dressed Asparagus next to rice.

Note: Chicken needs more time than the veggies to cook, so make sure to stir-fry well before adding vegetables. Otherwise, you'll end up overcooking the green pepper and bamboo shoot.

Side Dish: Plum Dressed Asparagus

Shred one pickled plum (*umeboshi*) and remove pit. Peel tough ends of 3 stalks green asparagus and cut into 1 1/2" (3 to 4 cm) lengths. Boil asparagus in salted water, drain, and dress with shredded plum meat. Lightly sprinkle with soy sauce.

Chicken and Eggplant Stir-fry Bento

Add an accent of basil, cover and cook chicken thoroughly

Photo on page 33

Chicken and Eggplant Stir-fry

Ingredients

3 1/2 oz (100 g) boneless chicken thigh
2 eggplants (the small, slender Japanese or Italian kind)
1/2 clove garlic
Salt and pepper, to taste
Dash dried basil
1 light tsp soy sauce
2 tsp olive oil

Instructions

1. Remove fat from chicken and cut into bite-size pieces. Cut eggplant into 3/4" (2 cm) thick rounds, halving larger rounds if needed. Soak eggplant in salted water to remove bitterness. Mince garlic.
2. Add olive oil to a well-heated pan and add chicken and garlic. Season with salt and pepper and stir-fry until browned. Reduce heat to low and cover.
3. When chicken is cooked add eggplant. Use medium heat and stir-fry until eggplant is tender.
4. Season with basil and soy sauce.

Packing Tips: Serve with Fried Sweet Peppers. Garnish rice with sesame seeds and serve stir-fry separately, with sweet peppers on the side.

Note: You can use thyme or oregano instead of basil. Just be careful not to add too much when using dried herbs, or the dish will turn bitter. If you have fresh basil, that's even better. Chop it up and add to stir-fry for a fresh flavor.

Side Dish: Fried Sweet Peppers

Poke several holes into 5 to 6 sweet frying peppers. Add oil to a heated pan and stir-fry peppers over medium heat. Season with salt and pepper.

Chicken and Potato Curry Bento

Japanese-style curry has a delicious blend of seasonings

Recipe on page 37

It's kind of difficult to serve soupy curry in a bento box. But use curry powder as a seasoning, and the problem's solved. Add soy sauce for a flavor that goes great with rice, and use generous portions of chicken and potato for a filling dish. Boil ingredients before stir-frying to thoroughly cook both chicken and potatoes. Take the time to boil first, and you end up saving yourself some trouble. Quick preparation is a must when making bento.

**Chicken and
Potato Curry
+
Spinach Omelet
+
Bonito Flakes**

Boil first, then stir-fry!
It makes chicken and potato easy to cook and reduces your time in the kitchen

Photo on page 36

Chicken and Potato Curry

Ingredients
3 1/2 oz (100 g) boneless chicken thigh
1 potato
1/2 tsp curry powder
1 tsp soy sauce
Salt and pepper, to taste
White sesame seeds, to taste
2 tsp vegetable oil

Instructions
1. Remove fat from chicken. Peel potato. Dice both into 1 1/4"
   (3 cm) chunks.
2. Boil potato until soft enough to easily insert a skewer. Remove
   and set aside in a colander to drain. Add chicken to boiling
   water used for potato. Boil until cooked through and set aside
   in a colander to drain.
3. Add oil to a heated pan and stir-fry chicken and potato over
   medium high heat.
4. When ingredients are coated with oil, season with curry powder, salt, and soy sauce. Finish with sesame seeds.

Packing Tips: Serve with Spinach Omelet. Curry flavor is a great
match for eggs. Slice omelet into bite-size pieces and serve next
to curry stir-fry. Add a dash of soy sauce to bonito flakes and
place on rice for extra soy sauce flavor.

Note: Chicken needs more time than the veggies to cook, so
make sure to stir-fry well before adding vegetables. Otherwise,
you'll end up overcooking the green pepper and bamboo.

Side Dish: Spinach Omelet
Use 1/4 bunch spinach. Boil, then soak in lukewarm
water to remove bitterness. Squeeze out excess water
and chop finely. Blend white and yolk of 1 egg and
add spinach, 1/2 to 1 tsp sugar, and a dash of soy
sauce. Mix well. Add a pat of butter to a heated pan
and spread over pan surface quickly to avoid burning.
Pour in egg. Stir with large sweeping motions until
egg is half-done. Roll omelet to one side of the pan
and cook until surface is golden brown. Turn over and
cook opposite side. Use medium heat.

Satisfying Fried Fish Bento

As you may have noticed, the majority of recipes in this book are focused on meat. But that doesn't mean I'm not a fan of fish. Simmered or grilled fish dishes don't work very well in bento. But fried fish is another story. They have all the satisfying volume of a meat dish and a delicious, rich flavor that goes great with rice. Here I introduce a few fried fish bento recipes.

Fried Smelt
+
Sausage
+
Sesame Potatoes
+
Marinated Carrot
+
Japanese Pickles

Fried Smelt Bento

Fry dried fish for an excellent bento!

Recipe on page 40

Grilled fish doesn't really work for bento, but fish fried in hot oil is a welcome addition to the bento family. Frying brings out savory flavors, especially with dried fish like smelt. Just be careful to pat them thoroughly dry and dust with flour before frying, or they could burst open. Serve with marinated carrots, sausage and potatoes for a good and filling lunch.

Fried Smelt Bento

Start frying on low heat and finish on high—no worries if they pop open

Photo on page 38

Fried Smelt

Ingredients

4 to 5 smelt
Flour, for dusting
Oil, for deep-frying

Instructions

1. Press fish with paper towels and pat completely dry. Dust evenly with flour and grip lightly to make it stick.
2. Heat 3/4" (2 cm) oil to medium high. (Check temperature by sprinkling with flour. If flour sinks halfway before rising up to the surface, oil is ready.) Add fish. Keep heat at medium low.
3. Fry fish slowly, turning occasionally. Raise heat to high before removing for a crispy finish.

Packing Tips: Serve with 2 boiled sausages, sesame potatoes, and marinated carrots. Top rice with a tangy Japanese pickle of your choice.

Side Dish: Carrot Marinade

Take 1/2 a carrot, peel and cut diagonally into thin rounds, then julienne. In a bowl, mix marinade (1/2 Tbsp olive oil, a pinch salt, pepper and lemon juice to taste), add carrot and marinate for 5 to 10 minutes.

Side Dish: Sesame Potatoes

Recipe on page 91

Fish and Chips Bento

**Make the batter flavorful and spicy—
for frozen potatoes, start frying from low heat**

Photo on page 42

Fish and Chips

Ingredients

1 cut fresh cod
Flour, for dusting
Batter:
  3 Tbsp each flour and water
  Dash each baking powder, salt, pepper and spices (chili powder, garlic powder, celery powder, nutmeg, etc.)
Frozen french fries
Oil, for deep-frying

Instructions

1. Remove skin and bones from cod fish and slice in half lengthwise. Coat with flour. Mix batter ingredients in a bowl and add fish. Coat well.
2. Fry potatoes first. Heat 3/4" (2 cm) oil in a pan and add frozen fries while oil is still lukewarm. Fry potatoes slowly, raising oil temperature gradually to medium heat.
3. When fries are done, keep heat at medium and stir oil with cooking chopsticks to slightly lower the temperature. Gently add batter-coated fish. Fry slowly, turning occasionally. Raise heat to high before removing for a crispy finish.

Seasoned Pike Bento

Marinate pike as you fry the veggies, and it'll be ready just in time

Photo on page 43

Seasoned Pike, Fried Sweet Potatoes and String Beans

Ingredients

1 small pike
Marinade:
> 1 light Tbsp each soy sauce, sake
> 1 tsp mirin (sweet cooking wine)
> Juice squeezed from grated ginger, to taste

Potato (or corn) starch, for dusting
1/2 sweet potato
3 to 4 string beans
Oil, for deep-frying

Instructions

1. Remove head and innards of fish, rinse well and wipe thoroughly dry with a paper towel. Chop into 1 1/4" (3 cm) pieces and soak in marinade for about 7 to 8 minutes.
2. Cut sweet potato into 1/2" (1.5 cm) thick rounds. Remove strings of string beans and cut in half.
3. Heat 3/4" (2 cm) oil to medium heat. Fry sweet potato first, frying slowly until a skewer can be easily inserted. Remove from oil. Next, fry string beans. Don't change oil temperature.
4. Drain fish well and coat with starch. Grip fish firmly to make starch stick and add to hot oil. Fry slowly on medium heat, turning occasionally.

Note: This bento is packed full of fried sides, so add a refreshing pickle to go with the rice.

Packing Tips: Make 3 rice balls with pickled plum (*umeboshi*) centers coated in sesame seeds. Pack a generous serving of fries and sprinkle with salt and pepper, if desired. Then add fried fish. Serve with broccoli boiled in salted water. As condiments for fish and chips, add ketchup, mayonnaise, and rice vinegar in small containers.

Note: Use whatever spices you have for the batter and season to taste. I recommend using chili powder.

Fish and Chips Bento

This British classic goes surprisingly well with rice balls

Recipe on page 40

This classic British dish works great as a bento. Naturally, freshly fried potatoes can't be beat, but even cold fries are a welcome treat in a bento box. The rice balls are a nice little refresher on the side. Carefully coat fish with plenty batter to prevent it from slipping off, and fry slowly.

Fried Fish
+
French Fries
+
Boiled Broccoli

**Seasoned Pike
+
Fried Sweet Potatoes
and String Beans
+
Japanese Pickle**

Seasoned Pike Bento

Marinate pike well for full flavor and no fishy odor

Recipe on page 41

Pike is most commonly served grilled. But soak it in sauce to remove odor and fry it, and you have yourself a great lunch box side dish. Soaking in sauce is essential. Go ahead and fry the vegetables on the side while the fish is soaking. Coat soaked fish with cornstarch and fry it good and crispy. If you have spare time, soak sweet potatoes in salt water before frying.

Bread Bento, Kentaro Style

An occasional bread-based bento is a welcome treat. You'll need volume to fill hard-working stomachs, but you can always use whatever ingredients or leftovers you have on hand. That's the advantage of bread bento!

Many of the sides served with rice in this book, such as Crumbly Curry and Salt-Grilled Chicken, go just as well with a slice of bread as with rice. When you use bread for bento, your options for fillings is unlimited. Japanese-style fried food like croquettes and fried pork cutlets are stomach-filling options. Eggs are great, too. Easy to cook with, endless potential for variety. You can make them into omelets, mix them with mayonnaise, scramble them, serve them sunny side up—the list goes on. Or try sautéing some veggies in olive oil. They're delicious and filling even when chilled.

Anything goes when it comes to sandwiches. That's what's so fun about them. Just slap whatever you want between two slices of bread. Add some cheese, and you're set to go. Add to that a thermos full of hot tea, and you have yourself a lunch that will bring back warm, fond memories for years to come.

Only thing to be careful of is using watery fillings that will make the bread soggy. But tomatoes go so well with bread, it's hard to resist adding them to a sandwich. Some people remove the slippery seed center, but that's the tastiest part, so I leave it in. What I do is pat tomatoes dry with paper towel and then protect the bread with a generous layer of butter. Butter and mustard or butter and ketchup are tasty options too.

Here's another idea: add a little jam and cream cheese sandwich on the side with some fresh fruit. That kind of sweet treat can be eaten as dessert or saved for an afternoon snack. Either way, it is sure to put a smile on their face.

Bread for lunch is great stuff, even if it's not the most typical thing to find in a bento box. Rice is the more traditional part of Japanese bento. But bread for lunch makes a nice change every now and then.

Layered sandwiches:
scrambled ham and egg,
tuna salad (tuna + minced
onion + mayonnaise + basil
+ pepper), tomato and
ham. Bread is lathered with
butter and mustard, and
sandwiched with lettuce.

45

Cheeseburger Bento

Shape it, grill it, pack it. American-style cheeseburgers make a great, easy lunch.

Recipe on page 48

No fillers whatsoever in this burger, just meat. Pat it into shape and grill it, that's the way I learned to do it. A 100% beef burger is plenty flavorful, and better yet, a cinch to whip up. All you have to do is grill it and slip it onto the bun. Highly recommended for bento. But do season with plenty of salt and pepper when grilling, as plain beef gets kind of boring.

**Hamburger
+
Lettuce
+
Sliced cheese
+
Sautéed onion
+
Pickles**

Seafood Salad and Baguette Bento

Looks light but it's surprisingly filling with a satisfying curry flavor

Recipe on page 48

Tartar sauce can make fish delicious even for those not very fond of seafood. Serve seafood salad and bread separately, for self-service sandwiching. Sauté fish, season with oregano, add chunks of boiled egg, pickles, onion, and cucumber, coat with tartar sauce. That's it. Finish with a pinch of curry powder, the secret seasoning.

Seafood Salad
+
Mini Tomatoes
+
Cheese

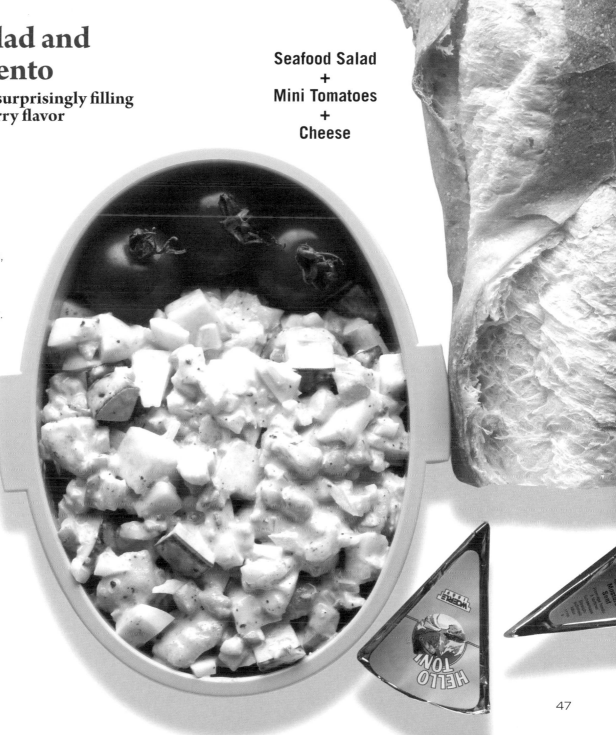

Cheeseburger Bento

Shape, fry, then sprinkle with salt and pepper.
Make the burger bigger than the bun.

Photo on page 46

Ingredients (Makes 2)
4 1/4 oz (120 g) ground beef
2 onion rounds (1/3" (7 mm) thick)
Salt and pepper, to taste
Vegetable oil
2 hamburger buns
2 slices cheese
1 to 2 whole pickles
1 leaf lettuce
Butter, mustard and ketchup, to taste

Instructions
1. First sauté onion. Add oil to a heated pan. Add onion rounds and lightly season with salt and pepper. Cook both sides on medium heat until lightly charred. Remove from pan and set aside.
2. Next cook burgers. Add oil to a well-heated pan. Divide meat in half and shape into thin patties. Quickly add patties to pan and season with plenty salt and pepper. Cook both sides until lightly charred, using medium high heat. Reduce heat and cook through.
3. Slice open hamburger buns and spread butter and mustard. Fill each bun with 1/2 leaf lettuce, burger, sliced cheese, sautéed onion, ketchup, and thinly sliced pickles. The order of ingredients is up to you.

Seafood Salad Bento

First cook fish, then mix. Soak onions in water.

Photo on page 47

Ingredients
3 1/2 oz (100 g) cod fish fillet
1 1/2 tsp olive oil
Dried oregano
Salt and pepper, to taste
1 egg
1/4 small onion
1/2 cucumber
1 whole pickle
Tartar Sauce:
⌐ 1 Tbsp mayonnaise
│ 1 tsp mustard
│ Dash each salt and pepper
└ Dash curry powder

Instructions
1. First sauté fish. Add olive oil to a well-heated pan and sauté fish on medium heat. Season with salt and pepper, turn and cook well on both sides. Sprinkle oregano. Hard-boil egg.
2. Mince onion and soak in water. Finely chop boiled egg. Remove stem of cucumber and quarter lengthwise. Dice into 1/3" (8 mm) cubed pieces. Dice pickle to similar sized cubes.
3. Remove skin and bones of cod and shred meat into a bowl. Add well-drained onion, boiled egg, cucumber and pickle. Combine with tartar sauce ingredients in bowl and mix well.

Packing Tips: Pack seafood salad and mini tomatoes together in an air-tight container. Slice open the baguette and wrap in paper. Add a wedge of cheese for a well-rounded lunch.

Note: Oregano is a handy and easy-to-use spice. Usually used to season tomato sauce, it also goes great with fish dishes like this one, so it's definitely good to keep on hand. Dry spices can be on the strong side, so don't go overboard when sprinkling.

Omelet and Hot Dog Bento

Whip up whatever's in the fridge, and you're on your way!

I highly recommend using a sausage-style hot dog. Grill it in a toaster oven or boil it. Sausage goes great with a deluxe omelet-dog packed full of fun fillings. Since the omelet is for a bento box, cook it well. You don't want gooey egg dripping all over the place. Use whatever you have on hand for the filling. Here I use avocado and to-mato. Add a pat of butter, a dollop of mustard and ketchup to taste.

**Sausage,
Avocado Omelet Dogs**

Ingredients

1 large sausage
Avocado omelet:
- 1 egg
- 1/2 avocado
- 1/2 tomato
- 1 slice bacon
- Salt and pepper, to taste
- Dash vegetable oil

Butter, whole grain mustard and ketchup, to taste
2 hot dog buns

Instructions

1. Cook sausage by boiling or by toasting in a toaster oven.
2. Make omelet. Peel avocado and dice into 3/4" (2 cm) cubes. Repeat with tomato. Cut bacon into 2/5" (1 cm) pieces.
3. Place bacon in pan and cook on low heat until crispy. Add a little oil and turn heat to medium.
4. Beat egg just enough to blend white and yolk and season with salt and pepper. Add to pan. Add avocado and tomato and stir with broad strokes. When egg is half-done, fold towards one edge, cook through, and flip. This can be done easily by using a dish to cover pan and turning upside down.
5. Slice hot dog buns lengthwise and butter. Add mustard to bun to be used for sausage. Sand-wich sausage and omelet each in a separate bun and serve with a ketchup packet.

Two Meals in One: Cooking with Leftovers

Turning leftovers into lunch is a master technique in the world of bento. To achieve your black belt in leftovers for bento, transform last night's dinner into a completely new dish with a little cleverness. It defeats the purpose, though, if it takes just as much time as cooking something from scratch. Here I introduce some outstanding recipes where you just set aside a little dinner and remake it into a refreshingly new dish the next morning.

Croquette in Simmered Egg Sauce
+
Nori
+
Red Pickled Ginger

Simmered Croquette Bento
Irresistibly delicious croquettes soaked in sauce

This recipe takes a favorite rice bowl recipe and turns it into lunch in a box. Use leftover potato croquettes or hash browns, either handmade or store-bought. By simmering in egg sauce, you can make it look and taste like a satisfying new treat. For greens use shredded cabbage. Just be careful to cook egg thoroughly. Half-cooked won't do for bento.

By all means, serve that croquette on rice. When lunchtime rolls around, the rice will be steeped in delicious simmering sauce!

Ingredients (Makes 2)
1 potato croquette (see below) (or hash brown)
Shredded cabbage, to taste
1 egg
Simmering sauce:
⌐1 Tbsp each soy sauce, mirin
└(sweet cooking wine), sake and water

Instructions
1. Combine simmering sauce ingredients in a shallow pan and bring to a boil.
2. Add shredded cabbage and boil again. Place croquette in center of pan.
3. When sauce is at a low bubbling boil, lightly beat egg and pour evenly over croquette. Cover immediately and cook on low heat until egg is done.

Packing Tips: Break up nori seaweed into fine pieces and cover rice. Top with croquette and cabbage cooked in egg sauce. Add red pickled ginger on the side.

Note: Usually donburi are served with creamy half-cooked simmered egg sauce, but for bento, cook egg thoroughly. To do this, leave heat on low after covering.

Reference Recipe:
Potato Croquettes
Combine equal parts of dry mashed potato and ground beef sautéed with minced onion. Season with salt and pepper and shape into patties. Coat with flour, beaten egg and breadcrumbs, in that order. Fry until golden brown and crispy. In Japan, deep-fried dishes are usually served with shredded cabbage to aid digestion.

Chicken *Sukiyaki* Bento

Add chicken to leftover *sukiyaki* from the night before!

Sukiyaki, a popular dish of skillet-simmered beef and vegetables, is chock full of delicious meat and veggie juices. So put that luscious leftover broth to good use. The beef is sure to be gone, so refill with some chicken. This kind of amazing flavor is precisely what makes leftovers for bento so luscious.

Ingredients

2/3 C sukiyaki broth
   (see Reference Recipe)
5 1/4 oz (150 g) chicken thigh
Garland chrysanthemum
   (or sub. spinach)
1/2 pack *shimeji* (clamshell)
   mushrooms
1/2 bundle *shirataki* (konnyaku)
   noodles

Instructions

1. Remove fat from chicken and slice thinly.
2. Blanch *shirataki* noodles in boiling water and cut to desired length. Remove stems of *shimeji* mushrooms and break into small clusters. Cut chrysanthemum into bite-size pieces.
3. Strain *sukiyaki* broth and bring to a boil in a pan. Add chicken and simmer. If you don't have enough broth, add water, sugar, soy sauce and mirin to taste.
4. When chicken is cooked, add *shirataki* noodles and *shimeji* mushrooms. Cook until noodles absorb broth, then add chrysanthemum leaves. When chrysanthemum is tender you're set to make the bento.

Packing Tips: Top rice with *sukiyaki* simmered ingredients, draining broth well. Serve red pickled ginger on the side.

Note: Chicken takes time to cook well. Slice thinly.

Reference Recipe:
The flavor of sukiyaki broth is up to you, but for your reference, my household uses the following Kansai-style (Western Japan) recipe: Sauté onions and beef in a large skillet. Add sugar, mirin and soy sauce to taste. Add vegetables. Add extra ingredients and seasonings as necessary while eating.

Slice chicken thinly
for quick cooking.
If the broth is too
thick, add water!

Chicken
+
Chrysanthemum
+
Shirataki
+
Red Pickled Ginger

Meatball Bento

Turn leftover hamburger into meatballs

Make an extra hamburger patty at dinner, and you can use it in a bento the next day. But instead of doing hamburger twice in a row, turn it into tasty Chinese-style meatballs. You can transform a Western meal into an Oriental treat, just by adding sesame oil and soy sauce.

Fried Meatballs

Ingredients

3 1/2 to 5 1/4 oz (100 to 150 g)
   hamburger patty (see next page)
Dash sesame oil
1/2 Tbsp soy sauce
Flour, for dusting
Oil, for deep frying

Instructions

1. Add sesame oil and soy sauce to uncooked hamburger patty. Knead well.
2. Prepare some flour in a shallow dish. Pull off chunks of hamburger and roll into 1 1/4 to 3/4" (3 to 4 cm) balls. Place in flour dish and coat thoroughly.
3. In a pan, heat 3/4" (2 cm) oil over medium low heat. Gently add flour-coated meatballs and fry slowly until crispy. Meatballs are done when no cloudy liquid comes out when poked with a skewer.

Packing Tips: Serve meatballs with Soy Sauce Potatoes and fresh boiled green asparagus. Use 3 to 4 stalks of asparagus and peel tough stem end before boiling. Cut into pieces and pack.

Note: If you fry on high heat, you are likely to get burnt outsides with raw insides. Using low heat and cooking slowly is essential. To check oil temperature, sprinkle some flour. If it sinks to the bottom and slowly rises to the top, temperature is medium low (275 to 300°F (140 to 150°C)). If flour rises immediately to the top, the temperature is too high (360 to 375°F or 180 to 200°C). In this case, stir oil to lower the temperature. Sometimes you have to turn off the heat. Use your instincts. It just takes a little getting used to.

Side Dish: Soy Sauce Potatoes

Peel and quarter 1/2 large potato and boil until cooked through. For sauce, combine 1 Tbsp each mayonnaise and soy sauce and add a dash of sesame oil. Drain potato well, add to sauce, and stir to coat.

When frying, remember:
Even if you're in a hurry, don't take shortcuts.
Start with low heat and take your time.

Fried Meatballs
+
Boiled Asparagus
+
Soy Sauce Potatoes

Reference Recipe:

Hamburgers

Ingredients (Serves 4)

10 1/2 oz (300 g) ground beef
1 3/4 oz (50 g) ground pork
1/2 onion
1 C breadcrumbs
1/5 C (50 ml) milk
1 egg
1/2 tsp salt
Dash pepper
1/2 tsp vegetable oil

Instructions

1. Mince onion and sauté until tender. Let cool.
2. Add milk and egg to breadcrumbs and mix well.
3. Add ground meat to a bowl and season with salt and pepper. Add sautéed onion. Lightly coat hands with oil and mix meat mixture. Add breadcrumb mixture and combine. Divide into 4 parts and shape into patties, pressing out excess air. See page 75 for cooking instructions.

Oden
+
Salted Daikon Leaves

When serving simmered foods for lunch, drain extra liquid well. Rule #1 in Bento Law.

Oden Bento

A one-pot dish, simmered in sauce then served for lunch

Oden is a simmered dish that's a popular wintertime treat and, as a rule, made in large quantities. That makes it a great leftovers-for-lunch candidate. However, the subtle flavor of *oden* isn't suited to being eaten cold for lunch, so season with extra soy sauce.

Oden

Ingredients

Oden fillings:
  Daikon, fish cake (*chikuwa*), *konnyaku* (konjac jelly), taro (or parsnips), fish dumplings, etc. (see Reference Recipe)
2 tsp each soy sauce, mirin (sweet cooking wine) and sake

Instructions

Remove *oden* ingredients from broth, cut into bite-size pieces and place in a pan. Add seasonings and cook on high heat.

Packing Tips: Serve separate from rice. On the side, serve Salted Daikon Leaves with baby sardines added. Make daikon leaves ahead of time and serve on cold rice.

Side Dish: Salted Daikon Leaves
Recipe on page 94

Reference Recipe:
Each household has their own favorite *oden* recipe. Here is the recipe we love: Soak 8 to 10 dried sardines (*niboshi*) and 6" (15 cm) *konbu* kelp in 6 1/2 C water. Bring to a boil and add a handful of dried bonito flakes, simmer 2 to 3 minutes, then strain. Add seasonings (1 Tbsp sugar, 1 tsp salt, 1 Tbsp each soy sauce and light soy sauce) to broth and then add fillings. Simmer until cooked.

Firmly press starch into the eel

Fried Eel
+
Fried Sweet Peppers
+
Japanese Pickle

Fried Eel Bento

Love that robust soy sauce flavor

Okay, so I admit that *kabayaki*-style eel is not likely to be leftover until the next morning. But this bento is so good, you really must try it. It's almost a waste to save this exceptionally delicious crispy fried flavor for lunch. It would make a good appetizer with an evening glass of sake, too. Anyways, try finding a venue that sells *kabayaki* eel cheap, so you'll have an excuse to buy extra and try this lip-licking leftover dish.

Fried Eel

Ingredients
1 filet *kabayaki* (barbeque) eel
Dash soy sauce
Potato (or corn) starch, for dusting
Oil, for deep-frying

Instructions
1. Cut eel into 1 1/4" (3 cm) pieces, sprinkle with soy sauce, and mix.
2. Place starch in a shallow dish and add eel. Coat well.
3. Heat oil to high and add starch-coated eel one piece at a time, gripping firmly before frying

Side Dish: Fried Sweet Peppers

Poke several holes in 4 to 5 sweet frying peppers to keep them from bursting. Fry in hot oil. While still hot, coat in soy sauce and add a drizzle of sesame oil. Finish with white sesame seeds.

Packing Tips: Let fried eel cool before packing. Eel may also be served on top of rice. Add a small serving of Japanese pickles on top of the rice.

Crispy Dumpling Bento

Just toast 'em—easier than frying and no pots or pans needed

It's easy to make extra when cooking dumplings, so they come in handy as sides for lunch. The usual trick is to deep-fry *gyoza* pot stickers, and the same can be done with steamed *shumai* dumplings, too. But here I introduce an even easier and just as tasty alternative: toasting those little dumplings in a toaster oven. To get them good and crispy, just coat with oil. That's all there is to it.

Crispy Chinese Dumplings

Ingredients

Shumai dumplings (see Reference Recipe)
Vegetable oil, as needed

Instructions

1. Keep leftover steamed *shumai* dumplings in the refrigerator overnight. Let cool before refrigerating.
2. Line toaster oven tray with aluminum foil and thinly coat with oil.
3. Arrange dumplings on foil and use a pastry brush to coat with oil. If you don't have a pastry brush, you can use a paper towel or a spoon.
4. Toast until crispy.

Packing Tips: Serve dumplings and side dish separately from rice.

Note: You can use store-bought *shumai* dumplings, but I recommend making them from scratch. See Reference Recipe.

On busy mornings, use toaster, a pan and a pot to cook three things at once.

Side Dish: Rolled *Mentaiko* Omelet

Lightly beat 1 egg. Add 1 tsp sugar and a dash of salt and mix well. Cut a 1 1/2" (3 to 4 cm) piece *mentaiko* (pollock roe) and crumble. Add a dash of sesame oil to a heated skillet or frying pan and pour in egg. Cook until half done, add crumbled mentaiko and roll omelet, wrapping roe inside.

Side Dish: Cabbage with Bonito Flakes

Recipe on page 94
One of the sides should be a freshly boiled vegetable. Spinach with Nori Seaweed (recipe on page 85) would also work well in place of cabbage.

**Crispy Chinese
Dumplings
+
Cabbage with
Bonito Flakes
+
Rolled *Mentaiko*
Omelet
+
Pickled Plum**

Reference Recipe:
Homemade *Shumai* Dumplings

Ingredients (Makes 30)
30 wonton wrappers
10 1/2 oz (300 g) ground pork
1/2 onion
3 Tbsp potato (or corn) starch
1 tsp each salt and sesame oil
Dash pepper
1 to 2 cabbage leaves

Instructions
1. Mince onion, add starch and mix well.
2. Add pork, salt, sesame oil and pepper to onion. Mix well by hand until sticky.
3. Wrap meat mixture tightly in wonton wrappers. Line a heated steamer with cabbage leaves. Place dumplings on top and steam for 10 to 15 minutes.

Bring on the Hefty Bento

Usually the word "bento" brings up images of rice served with several sides, but sometimes it's nice to have an all-in-one dish, main course and sides united together in delicious harmony. It makes things easier for the person making the bento, too. Just heap it on and you have a full bento box. Here I introduce some of my long-time favorites. Stir-fried Spaghetti, Three-Color Rice, Crumbly Curry—the list goes on.

Stir-fried Spaghetti Bento

Fried spaghetti doesn't clump when cold

Recipe on page 62

When I was a kid I used to love finding a heaping serving of *yakisoba* in my bento box. Imagine my surprise when I found out years later that my mother was actually serving us stir-fried spaghetti! Neither my sister nor I ever suspected the switch, proof that spaghetti works just as well as the usual steamed Chinese noodles. Plus, spaghetti doesn't get sticky or clumpy when cold. Dried spaghetti keeps well and is easy to have on hand, too. I've got to hand it to my mother on this one.

**Stir-fried Spaghetti
+
Sausage
+
Red Pickled Ginger**

Stir-fried Spaghetti Bento

Spaghetti will be stir-fried so keep it close to al dente

Photo on page 60

Stir-fried Spaghetti

Ingredients

3 1/2 oz (100 g) spaghetti
1 3/4 oz (50 g) thinly sliced pork
2 cabbage leaves
2/5 to 3/4" (1 to 2 cm) carrot
Salt and pepper, to taste
2 tsp vegetable oil
Dash cracked white sesame seeds
Dash *chuno* sauce (or Tonkatsu or
    Worcestershire sauce)
1 sausage

Instructions

1. Boil spaghetti according to package directions in salted water. Noodles don't have to be perfectly al dente, but be careful not to overcook or they'll get sticky.
2. Cut pork and cabbage to bite-size pieces and slice carrot into thin rounds, then chop finely.
3. Add oil to a heated pan. Add pork and stir-fry until lightly browned. Add carrot. Stir-fry just until carrot is tender, then add cabbage. Stir-fry and season with salt and pepper.
4. Add drained spaghetti. If noodles need to be broken up, add some spaghetti broth (or water) and stir. Add cracked sesame seeds and *chuno* sauce and coat noodles well. Turn heat to high and stir briefly.
5. Make a lengthwise slice in sausage and grill in a toaster oven. Grilling in a pan is also okay.

Packing Tips: Fill bento box chock full of stir-fried spaghetti and serve topped with sausage and red pickled ginger. Red pickled ginger is a must for stir-fried noodles. You can save time by cooking sausage in a toaster oven while stir-frying noodles.

White Rice is Delicious

Which is why, in this book, I don't mess much with my rice. With the rare exception of dishes like fried rice and crumbly curry, the lunch boxes in this book feature plain white rice, because that's the best way to make the most of the meat. A heap of white rice paired with a healthy serving of beef or chicken—what an unbeatable combination. The purity of the rice is pivotal, so you'll want to be extra careful to keep simmered side dish juices from spilling onto those snowy grains. Let me give you a few tips from the chef's perspective: When stir-frying, stir constantly. Raise heat to high for a crispy finish. Drain oil thoroughly from fried foods, and drain all the water from boiled dishes. And a note about preventing spoiling: don't put the lid on the box until it's ready to go out the door. Letting it cool properly keeps it from going bad. Don't pack hot and cold sides simultaneously. Pretty basic yet important points to remember. It's a lonely battle, whipping up lunch in the early morning hours, and efficiency is key. Boil your veggies while stirring the main dish, and pack freshly steamed rice first to let it cool. Little tricks like this can cut minutes off your prep time and help you to conquer the morning rush. But if you're not the multi-tasking type, you can, of course, do things one at a time. It all tastes the same, but you may have to wake up early.

In this book, I made realistic dishes a priority, so there's no fancy tricks or special ingredients needed. I know what it's like to stand in the kitchen, but I empathize with the bento eater's carnivorous cravings for meat-filled bento. Meat, meat, meat—that's what filled my mind as I planned these recipes. But the finished product is chock full of vegetables. Guess I can't go without my greens after all. Ironic, huh? And it's not like I put them in there for nutritional balance or anything. They're there for the flavor. A bento filled with meat helps the veggies go down.

So put this book to use, hum along to yourself as you make these bento, and just imagine the delighted face on the luncher when the lid comes off that bento box.

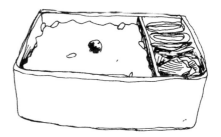

Spinach and Ground Meat Fried Rice

Meat, vegetables, and rice, all in a single bite!

Recipe on page 66

This brilliant fried rice dish has a healthy balance of meat and vegetables. You can use leftover boiled spinach, if you like, but be sure to use plenty. This dish would make Popeye proud. If you're using freshly cooked rice, let it cool first. If it's too sticky, stir-frying is difficult. You can solve that by spreading rice out in a vat or shallow dish. If you haven't the time to wait for it to cool, try sticking it in the freezer while you're stir-frying.

**Spinach and
Ground Meat
Fried Rice
+
Sausage
+
Curried Cauliflower**

Crumbly Curry Bento

This dish really makes rice delicious. A definite must-try!

Recipe on page 66

This deluxe crumbly curry dish is the pride of my household, packed with a variety of ingredients and full of flavor. Add a little Worcestershire sauce and sugar to accentuate the curry flavor. The original recipe calls for tumeric and bay leaf, too, but I omit those here. The key to well-seasoned beef is in the timing: add the spice just as the meat is on the verge of browning. Be sure to cook well after seasoning.

Crumbly Curry
+
***Fukujin* Pickle**

Three-Color Bento

Moist chicken straight from my mother's recipe book

Recipe on page 67

My mother's recipe for seasoned ground chicken is special because of its soft and tender texture. Needless to say, there's a good reason behind that. If the meat is too dry and crumbly, it falls off when you try to scoop it up with chopsticks, making it hard to eat. But moist and tender meat melds with rice and melts in your mouth. My mother Katsuyo is one clever lady. To achieve her special brand of tenderness, mix chicken and simmering broth well and leave a little sauce when cooking. For scrambled egg, use 5 chopsticks at once and whisk away.

Seasoned Chicken
+
Scrambled Egg
+
String Beans
+
Red Pickled Ginger

Spinach and Ground Meat Fried Rice Bento

If using freshly cooked rice, chill before stir-frying

Photo on page 64

Spinach and Ground Meat Fried Rice

Ingredients

2 servings rice
1/2 bunch spinach
2 1/2 oz (70 g) ground meat
1/2 clove garlic
Dash each salt, pepper and soy sauce
1 tsp each vegetable oil and butter

Instructions

1. If rice is still warm, spread in a shallow dish or vat to cool. If needed, place in the freezer.
2. Blanch spinach in boiling salted water, then soak in cold water to remove bitterness. Squeeze out excess water well and chop finely. Mince garlic.
3. Add oil to a well-heated pan and add butter. Sauté garlic until fragrant and add meat. Stir-fry over medium heat.
4. When meat is browned, add spinach and rice. Stir-fry well, breaking up any clumps. Season with salt, pepper and soy sauce.

Packing Tips: Serve with boiled sausage and Curried Cauliflower. Save time by boiling sausage and cauliflower together.

Side Dish: Curried Cauliflower

Recipe on page 91

Crumbly Curry Bento

Curry with Worcestershire sauce and sugar make this dish truly delectable

Photo on page 65

Crumbly Curry

Ingredients

3 1/2 oz (100 g) ground meat
1/2 green bell pepper
1/2 small stalk celery
1/2 clove garlic
1/2 nub ginger
1 tsp curry powder
1 tsp soy sauce
1 tsp Worcestershire sauce
Pinch sugar
Salt and pepper, to taste
2 tsp vegetable oil

Three-Color Bento

The trick to tender, crumbly chicken is simmering on low, leaving some sauce, and turning off heat

Photo on page 65

Instructions

1. Remove seeds and stem of bell pepper and mince. Mince celery, garlic and ginger.
2. Add oil to a lightly heated pan and sauté garlic and ginger over low heat until fragrant. Add ground meat and turn heat to medium. Stir-fry. Add bell pepper and celery and stir-fry just until meat is almost browned. Quickly season with curry powder, soy sauce, Worcestershire sauce, and sugar, in that order.
3. When meal is browned, check flavor and add salt as necessary. Finish with freshly ground pepper.

Packing Tips: Serve a heaping helping of rice and top with a healthy serving of crumbly curry. Serve pickles on the side.

Seasoned Chicken, Scrambled Egg, String Beans

Ingredients

[Seasoned Chicken]
3 1/2 oz (100 g) ground chicken
Simmering broth:
- 1 light Tbsp each soy sauce and mirin (sweet cooking wine)
- 1/2 nub ginger, grated
- 3 Tbsp water
- 1/2 tsp sugar

[Scrambled egg]
1 egg
1/2 tsp sugar
Pinch salt
1 tsp water
Dash sesame oil

[String Beans]
5 string beans
Pinch salt

Instructions

1. Make seasoned chicken. In a pan, mix chicken and broth well before cooking. Cook over medium low heat until chicken is browned, and stir to prevent clumping. Turn off heat before all broth has cooked off.
2. Make scrambled egg. Combine lightly beaten egg, seasonings, and sesame oil in a new pan and turn heat to low. Grasp 5 chopsticks at once and whisk vigorously to avoid burning until well-scrambled and crumbly.
3. Make string beans. Remove strings and boil in salted water. Slice thinly on the bias.

Packing Tips: Add rice to bento box. Top first with seasoned chicken, then scrambled egg, and finally string beans. Arrange each "color" neatly on top of the rice. Serve with red pickled ginger.

Note: The "green" in three color bento can be snow peas, green peas or boiled bell peppers. However, keep in mind that it goes on top of rice, so avoid leafy greens like spinach or *komatsuna*, as they might make rice watery.

Mentaiko Rice Bento

Just mix together for an effortless yet tasty lunch

Recipe on page 70

This is a dish that is super easy. All you have to do is mix rice and *mentaiko* (marinated pollock roe). Mix with bold, slicing strokes. Beware of stirring too much, or rice will get gooey. Check the flavor as you mix, but err on the bland side. If it's just right with the first bite, by the time you finish, it will be too strong to stomach. Don't forget to add an accent of *shiso* leaves and fragrant sesame seeds.

Mentaiko **Rice**
+
**Cucumber
Chicken Salad
with Plum Dressing**

Egg and Fish Cake Rice Bento

Don't fry the rice, just mix it!

Recipe on page 70

It's easy to burn fried rice. Also, it can be too dry and crumbly to easily eat for lunch. So here I just fry the fish cake and egg and mix into plain rice. The flavor of the fillings can be fully enjoyed, the rice is moist and fluffy, and it's delicious even when chilled.

**Egg and Fish Cake Rice
+
Sesame-Sprinkled
Green Peppers
+
Red Pickled Ginger**

Boiled Salmon Rice Bento

Boil salmon and mix into rice for a dish that gets more delicious with time

Recipe on page 71

Don't grill salmon, boil it. Then break it up, season it, and mix into rice. Why boil it? The answer is simple. When grilled, the flavor gets fishy with time. But boiled salmon with sake, sesame oil and soy sauce has a lovely flavor that holds even when chilled. When breaking up to add to rice, aim for big, appetizing pieces.

**Boiled Salmon Rice
+
Salted Edamame
+
Fried Fish Cake**

Mentaiko Rice Bento

Watch out for over-mixing—mix as though slicing, with a chop, chop motion

Photo on page 68

Mentaiko Rice

Ingredients

2-3 servings rice
1/4 to 1/2 cake *mentaiko* (pollock roe)
2 *shiso* leaves (or basil or mint)
Dash white sesame seeds
Soy sauce, to taste

Instructions

1. Remove membrane of *mentaiko* and break apart. Shred *shiso* leaves.
2. Stir rice, *mentaiko*, *shiso* and sesame seeds with bold, slicing strokes. Season with a dash of soy sauce, checking flavor as you go.

Packing Tips: Add some meat on the side. Here I serve Chicken Cucumber Salad with Plum Dressing. Rolled omelets work well, too.

Side Dish: Chicken Cucumber Salad with Plum Dressing

Recipe on page 95

Egg and Fish Cake Rice Bento

Add fried egg and fish cake to rice—the ultimate easy solution to the burnt-rice dilemma

Photo on page 69

Egg and Fish Cake Rice

Ingredients

2 servings rice
1 egg
1 tube-shaped fish cake (*chikuwa*. Or sub. imitation crab stick)
1/2 bunching onion (or green onion)
1 Tbsp *sakura* shrimp (or salad shrimp)
Salt and pepper, to taste
Dash soy sauce
2 tsp sesame oil

Boiled Salmon Rice Bento

**Boiled salmon is refreshingly tasty—
the key is combining soy sauce and sesame oil**

Photo on page 69

Boiled Salmon in Rice

Ingredients

2 servings rice
1 filet raw salmon
Pinch salt
1/2 tsp each sake and soy sauce
1 tsp sesame oil
Black sesame seeds, to taste
Nori seaweed, crumbled

Instructions

1. Boil salmon in salted water. Drain in a colander and pat dry with a paper towel. Break into chunks and remove skin and bones.
2. Combine sake, soy sauce, and sesame oil in a bowl and add boiled salmon. Once flavor is absorbed, stir into rice. Mix in black sesame seeds and crumbled *nori* seaweed.

Packing Tips: Serve with simple sides, such as salted edamame and a helping of fried fish cakes.

Note: Cook salmon thoroughly. It'll be seasoned later so don't worry about over-boiling.

Instructions

1. Slice fish cake into 1/5" (5 mm) rounds and mince bunching onion.
2. Add sesame oil to a really well heated pan and stir-fry leek and fried fish cake. Use medium heat.
3. Beat egg and quickly pour into pan. When edges of egg bubble up, stir vigorously. Add *sakura* shrimp, salt, pepper and soy sauce, mix briefly, and turn off heat.
4. Add rice and mix well.

Packing Tips: Serve with Sesame-Sprinkled Green Peppers, but they can get watery, so keep them in a separate container. They may also be served to the side of the rice. Red pickled ginger is a must-have rice garnish.

Side Dish: Sesame-Sprinkled Green Peppers

Recipe on page 86

Secretly Veggie-ful Bento Boxes

Kids are likely to be disappointed if they find a bento box full of green leafy things. So my solution is to serve them dishes that are filled with hidden vegetables. These dishes make the most of yummy veggie flavor, satisfy empty stomachs, and go great with rice. The vegetables are in hiding, but still make an impact.

Cabbage Cutlet Bento

Two leaves of cabbage make a satisfying fried cutlet

Recipe on page 74

The only ingredient other than cabbage is ground pork. Some pork and a whole bunch of chopped cabbage. Rub cabbage with salt and squeeze out liquid to keep cutlets from crumbling when fried. Mix meat and cabbage well. You don't need any extra ingredients to get the mixture good and gooey for shaping into patties. Serve cabbage on the side, too. Salted cabbage, in this case. Enjoy the versatility of cabbage.

**Cabbage Cutlet
+
Salted Cabbage
+
Japanese Pickles**

Cabbage Cutlet Bento

Be sure to mince cabbage finely, rub with salt, and squeeze out excess water well

Photo on page 72

Cabbage Cutlet

Ingredients (Makes 2)
2 cabbage leaves
2 1/2 oz (70 g) ground pork
Salt and pepper, to taste
Batter:
⌈ Flour, egg and *panko* breadcrumbs,
⌊ as needed
Oil, for deep-frying

Instructions
1. Remove core of cabbage leaves and slice into thin strips, then finely mince. Sprinkle with salt and rub. Let sit for 2 to 3 minutes to draw out moisture. Thoroughly squeeze out any liquid.
2. Mix ground pork and cabbage well by hand. Split mixture in half and shape into two small patties. Coat with flour, egg and breadcrumbs, in that order.
3. In a pan, heat 3/4" (2 cm) oil to medium low (140-150°C or 280-300°F) and gently slide in breaded pork cutlets. When crusts are golden brown check for doneness by inserting a skewer. If no cloudy liquid comes out they're ready.

Packing Tips: You'll want to keep cutlets separate from rice. And be sure to wait for cutlets to cool before packing Salted Cabbage. Fried dishes go great with Japanese pickles. Here, I used a miso-flavored pickle.

Side Dish: Salted Cabbage
Roughly cut 1 to 2 leaves cabbage into bite-size pieces and place in a bowl. Rub in some salt and squeeze out excess water.

Beef + Veggie Burger Bento

Add boiling water, cover and steam

Photo on page 76

Beef + Veggie Burger

Ingredients (Serves 1)

2 oz (60 g) ground beef
1/2 small carrot
4" (10 cm) celery
1/4 green bell pepper
1 heaping Tbsp *panko* breadcrumbs
1 Tbsp milk
Salt and pepper, to taste
Dash vegetable oil
Sauce:
- 1 Tbsp ketchup
- 1 Tbsp Worcestershire sauce
- 1 tsp soy sauce

Instructions

1. Peel carrot. Remove stem and seeds of bell pepper. Dice carrot, green pepper and celery into 1/4" (7 mm) cubes.
2. Soak *panko* breadcrumbs in milk.
3. Add diced vegetables and breadcrumbs to ground beef and mix well. Season with salt and pepper. Shape into a small patty, squeezing out excess air.
4. Thinly coat heated pan with oil and add hamburger once oil is hot. Use medium heat. Halfway through, turn hamburger. When both sides are browned, add 2/5 C (100 ml) boiling water, cover, and steam over low heat.
5. Combine sauce ingredients. When water in pan evaporates, pour in sauce and coat burger well.

Packing Tips: Burger should be kept separate from rice and served together with a side dish. Top rice with *shiba* pickle. On the side, serve Sticky Potatoes and Broccoli and Ham Salad. Lightly flavored sides go well with sauce-coated burger.

Side Dish: Sticky Potatoes

Peel 1 potato and cut to bite-size pieces. Add potatoes to pan and boil until cooked. Discard water, cover pan, and rock over medium heat to evaporate excess water. Sprinkle with salt and mix.

Side Dish: Broccoli and Ham Salad

Recipe on page 91

Beef
+
Veggie Burger
+
Sticky Potatoes
+
Broccoli and Ham Salad
+
Shiba-style Pickle

Beef + Veggie Burger Bento

Crunchy carrot and bell pepper bring add dimension to this dish

Recipe on page 75

Everyone loves burgers. But this one is chock full of carrots and green peppers and takes delicious beef to a whole new level. Steam to cook; that way you don't have to worry about a raw center. Plus you get a juicy, light burger. Dice veggies into crunchy cubes for a toothsome texture. When coating with sauce, use high heat to keep from getting soggy.

Veggie-Filled Meatballs Bento

Knead well for moist and chewy chicken meatballs

Recipe on page 78

The robust flavor of these veggie-filled chicken meatballs is tops. The secret to the moist and chewy texture is starch. Coat boiled Napa cabbage with potato starch, and add more when mixing in the ground chicken. Make your meat balls a little squashed, not perfectly round. That makes it easier to cook thoroughly. Sprinkle with Japanese pepper if you happen to have some. Add baby sardines and sesame seeds to plain white rice.

Veggie-Filled Meatballs
+
Sautéed Bell Peppers
+
Baby Sardines
+
Pickled Plum

Veggie-Filled Meatballs Bento

Coat boiled Napa cabbage with starch

Photo on page 77

Veggie-Filled Meatballs

Ingredients (Makes 6 meatballs)

2 1/2 oz (70 g) ground chicken
2 leaves Napa cabbage
2" (5 cm) bunching onion
  (or green onion)
2 fresh shiitake mushrooms
2 Tbsp potato (or corn) starch
1/2 Tbsp each sesame oil and
  oyster sauce
1 Tbsp flour
Salt and pepper, to taste
Sauce:
  ⌈ 1 Tbsp each sake and water
  | 1/2 Tbsp soy sauce
  ⌊ 1/2 tsp sugar
Dash Japanese (*sansho*) pepper
Dash vegetable oil

Instructions

1. Blanch Napa cabbage and mince. Squeeze out excess water and mix in 1 Tbsp starch. Mince bunching onion and shiitake mushrooms.
2. Combine chicken and vegetables from step 1 and add salt, pepper, sesame oil, oyster sauce, flour and 1 Tbsp starch. Knead well by hand until very sticky. Break into 6 pieces and shape into small meatballs.
3. Thinly coat a well-heated pan with oil and arrange meatballs in pan. Cook on high heat until browned, then flip. Cook other side until browned, lower heat to medium, and cover to cook through.

4. Combine sauce ingredients and add to pan. Simmer and coat. Sprinkle with Japanese pepper or seven spice chili powder, if desired.

Packing Tips: Serve meatballs and bell peppers separately from the rice. Mix sesame seeds and dried baby sardines sprinkled with soy sauce into the rice. Garnish with a pickled plum.

Side Dish: Sautéed Bell Pepper

Use 1/2 green bell pepper with stem and seeds removed and cut lengthwise to 2/5" (1 cm) pieces. Sauté in a lightly oiled pan and season with salt and pepper. Green peppers may be cooked in same pan together with the chicken meatballs; just remove green peppers before adding sauce.

Spring Roll Bento

High heat makes spring rolls burst, so be sure to fry slow on low

Photo on page 80

Spring Rolls

Ingredients (Makes 3 spring rolls)

3 spring roll wrappers
1/3 oz (10 g) dried *harusame* (or saifun) noodles
1/4 pack bean sprouts
1/4 bunch garlic chives
1 1/4" (3 cm) carrot
1 fresh shiitake mushroom
1 3/4 oz (50 g) boiled bamboo shoot
1/2 nub ginger
1 3/4 oz (50 g) thinly sliced beef
A ⌈ 1 light tsp each potato (or corn) starch and
  ⌊ soy sauce
Simmering sauce ⌈ 1 Tbsp each soy sauce and water
  ⌊ 1/2 Tbsp sake
1/2 Tbsp potato starch
Dash vegetable oil
Flour, for pasting
Oil, for deep-frying

Mixed Tempura Bento
Drop batter-coated ingredients into hot oil
Photo on page 81

Carrot, Chicken, Bunching Onion and *Sakura* Shrimp Tempura

Ingredients (Makes 1 each)

1/2 small carrot
1/2 skinless chicken breast
4" (10 cm) bunching onion (or leek)
1 Tbsp *sakura* shrimp
  (or salad shrimp)
Tempura batter:
  3 Tbsp flour
  2 1/2 Tbsp water
  Pinch salt
Oil, for deep-frying
Sauce:
  1 Tbsp each soy sauce, mirin
    (sweet cooking wine), sake

Instructions

1. Peel carrot and julienne. Slice chicken thinly and combine with carrot in a bowl.
2. Cut bunching onion into rounds and combine with *sakura* shrimp in a separate bowl.
3. Combine batter ingredients and add half to each bowl of ingredients from steps 1 and 2. Mix well.
4. Heat 3/4" (2 cm) oil in a pan over medium heat. Scoop up mixed tempura with a spatula and gently slide into hot oil. Fry slowly, turning repeatedly. When tempura is golden brown turn heat to high and fry until crispy.

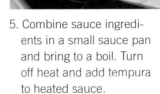

5. Combine sauce ingredients in a small sauce pan and bring to a boil. Turn off heat and add tempura to heated sauce.

Packing Tips: Place sauce-soaked tempura on top of rice and serve with *takuan* (daikon) pickle. Some people don't like *takuan* because of its strong odor, but for me, it is the best match for mixed tempura. You can replace it with another pickle if you like.

Instructions

1. Soak *harusame* noodles in water and cut to 2" (5 cm) lengths. Rinse bean sprouts and cut garlic chives to 2/5" (1 cm) pieces. Julienne remaining vegetables.
2. Cut beef to 2/5" (1 cm) strips and coat with mixture A.
3. Add oil to a well-heated pan and stir-fry beef. Add vegetables one by one starting with the hardest vegetables. Stir-fry over high heat. Add *harusame* noodles and simmering sauce. Stir. Pour in 1/2 Tbsp starch dissolved in 1 Tbsp water with a circular motion, and mix well to thicken sauce. Spread stir-fried ingredients out in a shal-

low dish and set aside to cool.
4. Add a little water to some flour to make a thick paste. Spread out spring roll wrappers and fill with ingredients from 3. Wrap up ingredients and use flour paste to keep wrapper edges firmly attached.
5. In a shallow pan, heat oil for deep-frying to 150°C (300°F) and gently slide in spring rolls. Fry slowly on low heat until golden brown then raise heat to medium high for a crispy finish. The filling is already cooked, and the wrappers will burst if fried at high heat, so don't use very high heat.

Packing Tips: Serve with light and refreshing sides: boiled broad beans and red pickled ginger. Cut spring rolls in half before packing for easy eating.

Note: To make spring roll wrappers easy to separate, wrap them in a moist towel until soft, then slap the towel to add air. They'll come right apart.

Spring Roll
+
Boiled Broad Beans
+
Red pickled ginger

Spring Roll Bento

A healthy bunch of meat and veggies all wrapped up

Recipe on page 78

Some might complain that spring rolls will lose their crispiness by lunchtime. But think about it. Sure, they take a little time and trouble to make, but I guarantee it's worth it. After all, you can still enjoy a filling treat like this and get plenty of veggies, even if the wrapper isn't perfectly crispy. Start with lukewarm oil and fry slowly. The fillings are pre-cooked, but if you use high heat right away they'll burst, so be careful.

Mixed Tempura Bento

Fried 'til crispy, veggies can make for a satisfying dish

Recipe on page 79

This mixed tempura have almost no meat or fish in them. This is where tempura shows its might. Meat or no, these crispy delights make popular bento sides. The secret to making them crispy is frying slowly to evaporate all that excess water. So use lukewarm oil and medium low heat, then soak in sauce. This technique works great for other fried sides, too. The veggies featured here are carrots and bunching onions. Feel free to add potato. Some dried sardines added to *sakura* shrimp also works.

**Carrot, Chicken,
Bunching Onion and
Sakura Shrimp Tempura
+
*Takuan***

Boiling is Best for Bento Boxes

Just boil it. Heat up some water, toss in the ingredients, and that's it. You're done.
You can whip up your sides while making the main dish.
Avoid watery sides with bento. When boiling, just remember to drain well.
And there's no worry about burning, since there is no frying involved.
You don't have to limit yourself to vegetables, either. Boil fish and meat too.
You'll get a flavor subtler than deep- and stir-fried meat cuisine,
which is just perfect for making them shine on the side of rice. By all means, boil away.

Boil Vegetables

How well you cook your vegetables is up to you, but in the case of boiling for bento go for a slightly firmer texture than usual so you can enjoy crispy veggies. Leafy greens especially will wilt later if boiled too long. Add salt to the water as necessary. That's the same as always.

Boil Meat and Fish

Boil meat and fish until well-done. Don't worry about overdoing it, especially as you're not going to burn anything. You may get some foam floating to the surface, but just skim it off when you're ready to remove your ingredients. A little salt is best when boiling fish, but nothing is needed for meat.

Drain in a Colander

Transfer your boiled ingredients to a colander right away and let them drain well. If necessary, pat dry with paper towel. Add seasonings while it's still hot for better flavor absorption. For ingredients that have been soaked in water, remember to squeeze out very well.

Bell Peppers in Oyster Sauce

Oyster sauce adds a rich flavor

Bell Peppers with Sesame Seeds

Simple soy sauce flavor with a hint of toasty sesame

Marinated Bell Peppers

Marinate after boiling— this dish gets more delicious with time

Bouillon-Boiled Red Bell Peppers

Boiling brings out pepper's sweetness

Boiled Snow Peas with *Sakura* Shrimp

Shrimp add color and calcium

String Beans with *Mentaiko*

Spicy *mentaiko* adds a tongue-tingling accent

Spinach with *Nori* Seaweed

The delicious aroma of shredded *nori* seaweed will whet your appetite

Spinach and Sausage Salad

Enjoy green vegetables in this sausage-enhanced salad

Bell Peppers in
Oyster Sauce

Photo on page 84, upper left

Ingredients

1 green bell pepper
Dash salt
1/2 tsp each soy sauce and oyster sauce

Instructions

Deseed bell pepper and cut into 1/5" (5 mm) strips. Blanch in boiling salted water. Drain well and season with soy sauce and oyster sauce.

Bell Peppers with
Sesame Seeds

Photo on page 84, upper right

Ingredients

1 green pepper
Dash salt
Sesame oil and soy sauce, to taste
Dash white sesame seeds

Instructions

1. Cut green pepper in half lengthwise and deseed. Slice widthwise to 2/5" (1 cm) pieces.
2. Blanch in boiling salted water. Drain well and while still hot season with soy sauce and sesame oil. Finish with white sesame seeds.

Marinated Bell Peppers

Photo on page 84, lower left

Ingredients

1/4 each red and yellow bell peppers
1/2 green bell pepper
Marinade:
 1/2 Tbsp each olive oil and rice vinegar
 Dash dried basil
 Pinch salt
 Dash pepper

Instructions

1. Deseed peppers and cut into 3/4 to 1 1/4" (2 to 3 cm) squares. Blanch and drain.
2. While still hot, soak in combined marinade ingredients.

Bouillon-Boiled
Red Bell Peppers

Photo on page 84, lower right

Ingredients

1 small red bell pepper
1/2 bouillon cube
Pepper, to taste

Instructions

1. Deseed bell pepper and slice lengthwise into thin strips.
2. Add bouillon cube to 1 C water in a pan and bring to a boil. Add bell pepper and boil briefly. Set aside to cool in the broth. Drain before adding to bento box and finish with pepper.

Boiled Snow Peas with *Sakura* Shrimp

Photo on page 85, upper left

Ingredients
10 snow peas
Dash salt
1 Tbsp *sakura* shrimp (or dwarf shrimp)
Dash each soy sauce and sesame oil

Instructions
1. Remove strings from snow peas and boil in salted water. Drain well.
2. Mix in shrimp. Lightly season with soy sauce and drizzle with sesame oil. Stir.

String Beans with *Mentaiko*

Photo on page 85, upper right

Ingredients
5 to 6 string beans
Dash salt
3/4" (2 cm) slice *mentaiko*
Dash each soy sauce and sesame oil

Instructions
1. Remove strings of string beans and boil in salted water. Drain in a colander and cut diagonally into thin slices.
2. Crumble *mentaiko* and mix with boiled string beans. Season with soy sauce and sesame oil.

Spinach with *Nori* Seaweed

Photo on page 85, lower left

Ingredients
1/2 bunch spinach
Dash salt
Toasted *nori* seaweed, to taste
Soy sauce, to taste

Instructions
1. Blanch spinach in boiling salted water and soak in lukewarm water to remove bitterness. Squeeze out well to drain and cut into bite-size pieces.
2. Sprinkle with shredded pieces of toasted *nori* and soy sauce.

Spinach and Sausage Salad

Photo on page 85, lower right

Ingredients
1/2 bunch spinach
Dash salt
2 sausages
Soy sauce and pepper, to taste

Instructions
1. Blanch spinach in boiling salted water and soak in lukewarm water to remove bitterness. Squeeze out well to drain and cut into bite-size pieces.
2. Cook sausage in a toaster oven (or frying pan) and slice into 2/5" (1 cm) thick pieces.
3. Toss spinach and sausage together and season with soy sauce and pepper.

Sweet Potato and Cream Cheese Salad

Cream cheese wraps around potatoes like a scrumptious sauce

Honey-Dressed Sweet Potato

Sometimes you just want a heart-warming sweet dish on the side

Cheesy Boiled Potatoes

Easy and delicious— cheesy flavor goes amazingly well with rice

Mentaiko Potatoes

The combination of pollock roe and potato makes for a great side dish

Curry-Marinated Cauliflower

Just boil and marinate—
curry flavor is truly delicious

Cheesy Potato Ham Salad

Three flavors in perfect harmony

Sesame Potatoes

Add a little soy sauce to
enhance the buttery flavor

Broccoli and Ham Salad

Add volume with the rich and
salty flavor of ham

Sweet Potato and Cream Cheese Salad

Photo on page 88, upper left

Ingredients
1/2 small sweet potato
2 Tbsp cream cheese
Raisins

Instructions
1. Peel sweet potatoes and cut into 1/2 to 3/4" (1 to 2 cm) rounds. Cover in water and boil until soft. Drain well.
2. Place sweet potatoes in a bowl and add cream cheese while sill hot. Mix well. Add raisins, if desired.

Honey-Dressed Sweet Potato

Photo on page 88, upper right

Ingredients
1/2 small sweet potato
Honey and cinnamon, to taste

Instructions
1. Cut unpeeled sweet potatoes into 2/5" (1 cm) rounds and then into halves. Boil, then drain.
2. Drizzle boiled sweet potato with honey and sprinkle cinnamon as desired.

Cheesy Boiled Potatoes

Photo on page 88, lower left

Ingredients
1 potato
Salt and pepper, to taste
1 Tbsp grated cheese

Instructions
1. Peel potatoes and cut into large chunks. Boil until soft.
2. Discard water and cover pan. Rock pan, cooking potatoes over medium heat until surface is powdery.
3. While potatoes are still hot, coat with salt, pepper and grated cheese.

Mentaiko Potatoes

Photo on page 88, lower right

Ingredients
1 small potato
1/4 cake *mentaiko* (pollock roe)
1 tsp mayonnaise
Sesame oil and soy sauce

Instructions
1. Peel potatoes and cut into small chunks. Cover in water and boil until soft. Drain water.
2. Place potatoes in a bowl and add crumbled *mentaiko*, mayonnaise, sesame oil and soy sauce. Mix well.

Curry-Marinated Cauliflower

Photo on page 89, upper left

Ingredients

1/2 head cauliflower
Marinade:
- 1/2 Tbsp each olive oil and rice vinegar
- Dash each salt, pepper and curry powder

Instructions

1. Break up cauliflower into clusters and boil. Drain in a colander.
2. Combine marinade ingredients and add boiled cauliflower while still hot.

Cheesy Potato Ham Salad

Photo on page 89, upper right

Ingredients

1/2 potato
1 3/4" (2 cm) thick slice American cheese
2 slices ham
1/2 Tbsp mayonnaise
Chili powder and pepper, to taste

Instructions

1. Peel potatoes and cut to 3/4 to 1 1/4" (2 to 3 cm) cubes. Boil until soft then drain.
2. Cut cheese and ham into 3/4" (2 cm) squares.
3. When boiled potatoes have cooled, mix together with cheese and ham and season with chili powder and pepper.

Sesame Potatoes

Photo on page 89, lower left

Ingredients

1 potato
Salt and pepper, to taste
Dash soy sauce
1/2 tsp butter
White sesame seeds, to taste

Instructions

1. Peel potatoes and cut into large chunks. Cover and boil until soft. Discard water. Rock pan, cooking potatoes over medium heat until surface is powdery.
2. Season potatoes with salt and pepper while still hot. Add butter and soy sauce, stir, and sprinkle with sesame seeds.

Broccoli and Ham Salad

Photo on page 89, lower right

Ingredients

1/2 head broccoli
Dash salt
2 slices ham
1/2 Tbsp mayonnaise
1 tsp wholegrain mustard
Pepper, to taste

Instructions

1. Break up broccoli into clusters and boil in salted water. Drain and set aside to cool. Cut ham into 1/2" (1 1/2 cm) squares.
2. Mix broccoli, ham, mayonnaise, mustard and pepper.

Recipes on Page 94

Plum Dressed Lotus Root

Perfectly tangy and
deliciously crunchy

Bacon and Asparagus

Get that bacon good
and crispy

Seasoned Carrots

Get the classic rich flavor
of *kimpira* without frying

Cabbage with Fish Flakes

Enjoy the cabbage flavor in this
delicious dish for all seasons

Salted Daikon Leaves

Blanched daikon leaves are
full of vitamin C

Recipes on page 95

Chinese-style Chicken

The secret to the unique flavor is in the soy-steeped sauce

Chicken and Cucumbers

The refreshing flavor of this meat-filled side is all thanks to the plum

Pork with Bacon and Mustard

A little pork on the side with mustard and bacon for flavor

Beef and Celery Salad

Make it in large quantities and it could be your main dish!

Wasabi Mayo Salmon

Wasabi packs a spicy bite that keeps your tongue tingling

Boiled *Mentaiko*

When you need just one more bite try this light and salty treat

Plum Dressed Lotus Root

Photo on page 92, upper left

Ingredients

1 3/4 to 2" (4 to 5 cm) lotus root
Dash rice vinegar
1 large pickled plum
Pinch dried fish flakes
Sesame oil and soy sauce, to taste

Instructions

1. Dice lotus root to 1/2 to 3/4" (1 to 2 cm) cubes and boil in water with vinegar. Drain well.
2. Mix boiled lotus root, shredded pickled plum, dried fish flakes, sesame oil and soy sauce.

Asparagus and Bacon

Photo on page 92, upper middle

Ingredients

3 stalks green asparagus
1 slice bacon
Dash soy sauce
Salt and pepper, to taste

Instructions

1. Peel tough skin on root end of asparagus and cut to bite-size lengths. Boil in salted water then drain well.
2. While boiling asparagus, cook bacon until crispy in an oven toaster or frying pan. Cut into bite-size pieces.
3. Mix boiled asparagus, crispy bacon, soy sauce, salt and pepper.

Seasoned Carrots

Photo on page 92, upper right

Ingredients

1/2 carrot
White sesame seeds, to taste
Dash each mirin (sweet cooking wine), sesame oil and soy sauce

Instructions

1. Peel carrot and cut into thin rounds and then chop. Boil.
2. Drain carrots well and mix with sesame, mirin, soy sauce and sesame oil.

Cabbage with Fish Flakes

Photo on page 92, lower left

Ingredients

1 cabbage leaf
Dash salt
Pinch dried fish flakes
Soy sauce, to taste

Instructions

1. Slice cabbage into 3/4" (2 cm) pieces and boil in salted water. Drain in a colander.
2. Mix with soy sauce and dried fish flakes.

Salted Daikon Leaves

Photo on page 92, lower right

Ingredients

Daikon leaves (from 1 daikon)
2 tsp salt
2 Tbsp baby sardines (*jako*)
White sesame seeds, to taste

Instructions

1. Chop daikon leaves and massage in salt.
2. Place in a colander and blanch by pouring boiling water over leaves.
3. Mince daikon leaved finely and sprinkle with extra salt, then mix in young sardines and soy sauce.

Chinese-style Chicken

Photo on page 93, upper left

Ingredients

1 chicken breast
1 1/4 to 1 3/4" (3 to 4 cm) bunching onion
   (or green onion)
1 Tbsp soy sauce
Dash sesame oil

Instructions

1. Mince bunching onion and place in a
   container. Pour in soy sauce and set
   aside.
2. Bring water to boil in a pan and add
   chicken. Drain well and shred chicken
   meat while still hot.
3. Add soy-steeped bunching onions to
   chicken, stir, and drizzle with sesame oil.

Chicken and Cucumbers

Photo on page 93, upper middle

Ingredients

1 chicken breast
1/2 cucumber
1 pickled plum
Soy sauce, to taste

Instructions

1. Boil chicken, drain, and shred. Set
   aside to cool.
2. Cut cucumbers into thin bars, sprinkle
   with salt to draw out water and pat dry
   with paper towel.
3. Combine chicken and cucumbers
   together with shredded pickled plum.
   Lightly season with a splash of soy
   sauce.

Pork with Mustard and Bacon

Photo on page 93, upper right

Ingredients

2 1/2 oz (70 g) thinly sliced pork
1 slice bacon
1/2 Tbsp wholegrain mustard
Salt and pepper, to taste

Instructions

1. Cut pork to bite-size pieces, boil,
   then drain.
2. While boiling pork, cook bacon in
   a toaster oven (or frying pan) until
   crispy, then chop.
3. Mix together pork, bacon, mustard,
   salt and pepper.

Beef and Celery Salad

Photo on page 93, lower left

Ingredients

1 3/4 oz (50 g) thinly sliced beef
2 to 2 1/2" (5 to 6 cm) celery
Pinch celery leaves
Dressing
   1/2 Tbsp each lemon juice and olive oil
   1 tsp soy sauce
   Salt and pepper, to taste

Instructions

1. Cut beef into bite-size pieces, boil, then
   drain.
2. Slice celery thinly to break up fibers.
   Mince celery leaves.
3. Combine dressing ingredients in a bowl
   and add beef, celery and celery leaves.
   Mix well.

Wasabi Mayo Salmon

Photo on page 93, lower middle

Ingredients

1 filet raw salmon
Dash salt
1 tsp wasabi
1 light Tbsp mayonnaise
Dash soy sauce
White sesame seeds, to taste

Instructions

1. Boil salmon in salted water. Remove
   skin and bones and finely shred meat.
2. Mix salmon, wasabi, mayonnaise, soy
   sauce and sesame seeds.

Boiled *Mentaiko*

Photo on page 93, lower right

Ingredients

1 cake *mentaiko* (pollock roe)

Instructions

Boil *mentaiko* until center turns light
pink. Cut and serve as desired.

Kentaro Kobayashi

Born 1972 in Tokyo, Japan. Kentaro began working as an illustrator while attending Musashino College of Fine Arts, and simultaneously put his inborn love of cooking to work by becoming a culinary artist. In addition to charismatically introducing recipes on television and in magazines, he helped develop ready-made recipes for retail sale and also hosted cooking classes, among other various activities. Kentaro's motto is "Easy and delicious, stylish yet realistic." In particular he proposes menus and meal plans based on what he himself wants to eat and make, in keeping with his lifestyle and the idea of always being practical. This book is written from that perspective and draws on the author's own personal experience.

Bento Love

Translation: Patricia Kawasaki
Vetting: Lisa Reilly

Copyright © 2009 by Kentaro Kobayashi
Photography © 2009 by Hideo Sawai

Published by Vertical, Inc., New York.

Originally published in Japanese as *Don to Genki Bento* by Bunka Shuppankyoku, Tokyo, 1998.

ISBN 978-1-934287-58-3

Manufactured in The United States of America

First American Edition

Vertical, Inc.
www.vertical-inc.com